BECOMING
AN EMBEDDED
LIBRARIAN

BECOMING AN EMBEDDED LIBRARIAN

Making Connections in the Classroom

MICHELLE REALE

An imprint of the American Library Association

CHICAGO 2016

MICHELLE REALE is an associate professor at Arcadia University at Glenside, Pennsylvania, where she is a fully embedded librarian. She divides her time between the United States and Sicily, where she does ethnography among African refugees. She blogs on immigration, migration, and social justice in the Sicilian context at www.sempresicilia.wordpress.com.

ISBNs
978-0-8389-1367-3 (paper)
978-0-8389-1375-8 (PDF)
978-0-8389-1376-5 (ePub)
978-0-8389-1377-2 (Kindle)

Library of Congress Cataloging-in-Publication Data

Reale, Michelle.
   Becoming an embedded librarian : making connections in the classroom / Michelle Reale.
      pages   cm
   Includes bibliographical references and index.
      ISBN 978-0-8389-1367-3 (paper : alk. paper) 1. Academic libraries—Relations with faculty and curriculum. 2. Academic librarians—Professional relationships. 3. Research—Methodology—Study and teaching (Higher) 4. Information literacy—Study and teaching (Higher) 5. Academic libraries—Reference services—United States—Case studies. 6. Libraries and colleges—United States—Case studies. I. Title.
      Z675.U5R44155 2016
      020.92—dc23   2015024587

Cover design by Alejandra Diaz. Images ©Rawpixel/Shutterstock, Inc.

Text composition by Dianne M. Rooney in the Chaparral, Gotham, and Bell Gothic typefaces.

♾ This paper meets the requirements of ANSI/NISO Z39.48-1992 (Permanence of Paper).

Printed in the United States of America

20 19 18 17 16   5 4 3 2 1

Dedicated to embedded librarians everywhere.

Contents

DR. SANDRA CRENSHAW

Foreword

A View from the Lectern

I WASN'T QUITE SURE HOW TO REACT THE DAY THAT I FOUND OUT that there would be a librarian embedded in my senior seminar class the following semester. Should I be excited that there would be another academic voice to help guide the students in their research for their senior projects? Should I wonder if the addition to my class was an indication of the department's concern for my teaching? Would this be an added burden on my students? On me? Or worse yet, would it mean that everything—from syllabus to grading—would need to shift away from my comfort zone of control? I had heard of attempts to embed librarians in sections of the same course in previous semesters, and I knew that it had been tough going. It was clear that the faculty member didn't really know what to do with the librarian attending their class every week, and that the librarian was struggling to be an effective resource for the students because of this lingering question mark which everyone felt every day.

My first decision in the process was to not be *that* professor. That I would make this work . . . confident in my students' abilities to adapt to and appreciate the role of the librarian in our classroom, and confident in my own desire to learn from the experience and from my colleague. I knew it would mean taking on some new pedagogies and letting some go, being flexible in the classroom to a certain degree, and being hyper-aware of what a librarian can and should change in a classroom to make it better.

With trusty pen and paper, I met for the first time with Michelle about my section of the senior seminar class. We sat in her office talking. Five minutes turned to fifteen, which turned to thirty, which turned into ninety. We talked about the dynamics of classes with embedded librarians, how relationships between teacher and students are made more dynamic and complex than in traditional classrooms, and about how her voice might enhance the experience and assignments for the class. I'm happy to say that this was one of many meetings which we had in the following months, and I'm also happy to say that with every meeting, I grew more and more excited about the potentials.

We planned research assignments and discussed expectations. We talked about what would be ideal shifts and changes in the student experience and how this would enrich their writing. We even talked about how the students' relationships with me and with each other would develop into more complex, fulfilling dynamics in the classroom.

Then the day of reckoning came. *The first day of class.*

As we marched through all of those things you do on the first day, I introduced Michelle to the class as our "embedded librarian"—the authority on all things research-related, a source of support and solutions for their research struggles (which they always have, though many students won't admit it), and a dedicated sounding board for their projects. Michelle stood, and as I looked out at the faces of the students as she talked about her purpose and role, I saw a mixture of excitement, relief, shrugging apathy, and confusion (and maybe even fear?).

In that moment, it struck me. The students were imagining the same questions that I had when I first heard of Michelle's role in my class. I was looking in a mirror reflecting months ago, before I understood the role of embedded librarians in the classroom. Without expecting it, I had just drawn a bit closer to my students in that shared moment.

The consistent objective of every good professor in each course they teach is rather basic: to provide the students with the most effective learning environment for the course content, including considerations of pedagogies, materials, venues, and supports. Educational researchers have explored ways to accomplish this for decades, focusing on student-teacher relationships, co-curricular resources for struggling students, and even the effective placement of the trash can in the classroom setting. What many educational researchers sidestep, perhaps because it is difficult to quantify and harder to assess, is the nature of social connections in a college classroom and how they affect learning.

The traditional college classroom acknowledges only one major "social" connection, the relationship between the teacher and the students. Work is set forth by the faculty to create the faculty-produced objectives. Students work and achieve the objectives with primary guidance by the faculty and the course materials, even if students are encouraged to work together to solve a problem. The students' process and product, in the end, are foundationally based in the student-teacher relationship.

But such a simplistic social structure is fragile. If trust, enthusiasm, clarity, and communication are maintained between the teacher and students, the class runs smoothly. If any one of these characteristics fails, the relationship breaks down and the teacher becomes an outsider to the bonds already deeply forged between students. The permutations of such an exile in the classroom are many, and are difficult to recover from. Even in Freirian, decentered classrooms, the students' and teacher's trust and communication must withstand the stresses of the students' self-directed learning in order for it to be successful, thereby maintaining the structure of the student-teacher relationship while shifting its emphasis.

Social researchers who study complex networks suggest that a "community" is an organizational relationship structure which connects smaller, complexly connected groups (nodes) to each other through shared goals, objectives, experiences, and outcomes. In a college classroom, the students represent one node, while the teacher represents another. But what happens when a librarian resides in the classroom as well?

What happens is amazing. The shared struggles of the students, teacher, and librarian in establishing the new matrix of roles (nodes) and relationships in the classroom evolve into a more complex, stronger community, with more links among students (for their parallel experiences with the librarian), stronger links between students and teacher (for their shared experience with the new perspectives which the librarian brings to the objectives and content of the course), and ultimately, a richer classroom community which encourages student confidence and deeper thinking about skills and content.

This is not to say, however, that the new classroom community structure doesn't have its challenges. One of the greatest struggles for the faculty member is the self-reflective practice that must underpin the new, more dynamic classroom community structure. Where before the faculty might reflect generally about how the class went on a given day, the necessary discussion with the librarian before and after the class session lays bare the faculty's strengths and weaknesses, whether they are pervasive or just how this class turned out on that particular day. This discussion pokes at the edges of both the content and pedagogy, the construction and the relationships of the course. And that is a hard thing to explore for some, even for those who welcome the librarian into their classes. In effect, it means self-reflection, which is the first—and most uncomfortable—step in effective self-assessment (of both pedagogy and student learning).

And it's not an easy place for the embedded librarian to be, serving as the translator/negotiator between faculty and students, as well as a kind of translator/negotiator between what the faculty thinks they're doing pedagogically and what's actually happening in the classroom. But once communication and trust are established between faculty and librarian (and all the nodes of the community are clearly linked to each other through that communication and trust), the community of the class can stand on firmer ground.

So in the end, where does this leave us? Where did it leave my class, the students, me, and our embedded librarian?

On the last day of class, it left us with applause. But the fascinating thing was that the students weren't just applauding because they were done and had a well-deserved break looming in front of them. They applauded for themselves for tackling the content theory that had terrified nearly all of them at the start of the semester. They applauded me for helping them reach their goals. But most significantly, they applauded Michelle for being the solution to their frustration (both with their research and with my presentation of the content), for being the encouraging and guiding voice when they lost their way in the process, and for being what they always wanted (but never knew they wanted) . . . a mentor who helped them negotiate the content and process of their research and who was something different than the traditional, all-powerful, grade-bestowing faculty member.

That day, I also joined in the applause because I had found someone to challenge my stale ideas and uphold my good ones. I'd found a partner in the classroom community who bound us together in ways that helped me reach my goal of providing the students the most effective learning environment we could.

And I, for one, can't wait to do this again.

Acknowledgments

GRATEFUL AND HEARTFELT THANKS TO JAMIE SANTORO AT THE American Library Association for being not only the kindest and wisest of editors, but, as well, the most patient and encouraging. Without her belief that this book could take shape, it might not have happened. Thank you to Dr. Jeanne Buckley and my fellow librarians at Arcadia University with whom I had many rousing conversations about embedded practice, and for their support in my endeavors. To Maria T. Accardi, who has, in a thousand different ways, shown me how to enact my true and whole self in the practice of critical pedagogy in the classroom and to the many librarians who wrote wonderful books on embedded practice that helped to show me the way. And, as usual, to my wonderful family for supporting me in all of the important ways. I remember every kindness.

Introduction

*If you want something new, you have
to stop doing something old.*

—Peter F. Drucker

S O MUCH HAS BEEN WRITTEN IN RECENT YEARS ON THE CRISIS
of the identity of the librarian, the demise of the book (and therefore,
the library), as well as other dire predictions. One often feels as though it is
demanded of us information professionals to continually reinvent ourselves,
which is not necessarily a bad thing. We work in a profession that has been
historically misunderstood in just about every way conceivable. I have encountered my share of people who did not even know that a librarian needed a
master's degree! I have also encountered the assertion "my grandmother was
a librarian!" a few times.

Times change and professional practice changes with it. In academia,
librarians now, more than ever, are often seen as collaborative partners in
the education process, more so with the advent of designing, promoting, and
enacting information literacy. Librarians are now more active on campuses,
largely having shed our "auxiliary" role to faculty (but still recognizing and
fulfilling our role as research support) as we partake in committees, campus
governance, social events, and engaging in and presenting our own research.
This has helped faculty to see us as "partners" and "colleagues," and has shown
us to be active, involved, and engaged members of the campus community
with a common goal: the support and education of our *students*.

This change in our involvement is not mere cosmetics; it is real transformation. I have seen this in my own university library where just a mere ten years ago it would have been unheard of for me and my colleagues to be doing half of the things we are doing now (teaching, proposing classes, being elevated to professor status, etc.) simply because we were not seen as being capable or deserving of a seat at the table. Not true, of course, but perception is everything. With a new library director at the helm eight years ago, she had a plan that would elevate each and every one of us to faculty status. But she said it would take a while to get there: we should do our work and do it well. We began calling ourselves "faculty librarians," which at first confused and confounded faculty. "No matter," our director said. "Continue. It will make a difference." And she, in her proven infinite wisdom, was correct.

Over the years we entered into territory including but also beyond the reference desk that none of us could have imagined for ourselves. We worked slow and steady, but we took chances and became innovative with our practices. We promoted both ourselves and the library. We expressed discontent with the old way of doing things, but we did so in a constructive way: we proposed alternative ways of doing things. We tried different reference models, eschewing the "sit and wait" model of reference. We reasoned that how could someone respect a reference librarian who simply sat, just waiting all day for a question? We were on our way to being full faculty and wanted to be seen as such.

It was in this climate of great change and questioning that I began to feel a deep dissatisfaction with one-shot instruction, students who remained clueless after instruction, professors who dictated to me what to teach, when, and for how long, despite the fact that the subject I was teaching was my own specialty! As well, I lamented the lack of continuity with students. For sure, they could make an appointment with me if they needed to, but few did—so neither they nor I had the benefit of continuity. Since I was (and still am) the English department liaison, I decided to test the waters a bit with the courses required for the English major, in addition to Senior Thesis class.

One of the frustrations of doing bibliographic sessions in various classes is that the students are often not connecting, not absorbing what you are trying to teach them. As well, library and research "skills" are not highly prized— mainly, because skills are often seen as the opposite of what is considered academic. Forget the fact that in most places (my institution being one of them) we do not have a credited course on library skills implemented in the curriculum, nor do we otherwise grade or hold students accountable for what we have taught them. We rely heavily on faculty to reinforce the skills we have taught, but the truth is, that in many cases, professors are not well versed in the skills themselves and often have no particular interest in learning them.

The first year I was frustrated at every attempt to be a vital presence in the class. The professor, now retired, who taught thesis was reluctant to allow me to attend or participate in any more than two classes a semester, and was even resentful of that. He told me that his students knew what they were doing. I assured him that what we saw at the reference desk was in direct opposition to that. He took offense. He sighed heavily, telling me that he did not want to change a thing—he'd had a formula for this long and it seemed to work. Only, it didn't. So for the next two years, I worked trying to make inroads into other English classes, and while my "help" was always appreciated, I was hardly seen as integral to the students' learning. I even noted several times when I was clearly used as a "babysitter" of sorts—I would be asked to go to a class to do a "session" only to find out that the professor would not be in attendance. Those were difficult classes. Because I had been given no authority whatsoever, the students' attendance and attention span were poor. It was causing me to rethink my career. As clichéd as it sounds, I felt like Sisyphus, continually rolling that boulder up the mountain only to have it roll down again.

I had some of what I will call "tacit" knowing, some instincts about how I wanted my interactions and my teaching to go with students. I had a sense of what I could accomplish with them if I would only be given the chance. It was not until the professor who rebuffed my attempts to integrate information literacy into his class retired and two new professors were assigned to teach the Senior Thesis class that I jumped in with both feet.

I had just started reading about embedded librarianship and was incredibly intrigued (and excited) by the possibilities. I had read the positive and the negative, but the negatives, mostly the argument that librarians are librarians—not professors—did not dissuade me at all. In fact, I disagreed with the argument wholeheartedly—if librarians are not educators, then what are we?

I put together a proposal but not too thought out, because I felt that if the two professors were amenable to the idea, I would like the classes to be a collaborative effort. Friends of mine, professors and librarians alike, were skeptical of my approach, and felt that I was trying to stake out territory that was not mine for the taking. Misunderstood again. In fact, that could not have been further from the truth. What is true is that professors may feel threatened or territorial. That is only natural, most especially given the fact that fundamentally, a librarian's mandate is often (but thankfully not always) a totally mystery to faculty.

If necessity is the mother of invention, I felt the imperative to try something different. I have been embedded for a few years now in the Senior English Thesis course, two sections each fall semester. There have been pitfalls and missteps, for sure. All in all, it has been a process. Sometimes a maddening one, but often also transformational—for me and for my students.

When I tell people that I am an "embedded" librarian or that I have been "embedded" in classes within my liaison discipline, the reaction is usually one of confusion—from non-librarians and academics as well: "You're what? I'm sorry, can you explain that?" You know the old response to a joke that falls flat: *I guess you had to be there*. Well, that is how I came to being embedded in classes. As a librarian who began doing one-shot instruction and who felt early on and clearly that it did not work, neither for me nor for my students, I realized that I needed to know what they didn't know and I needed to know what they knew. In a very real and not figurative way, *I had to be there*. I realized that I had to be in class with the students, I had to hear what they were hearing and I had to be able to engage with them there in order to be of any help to them at all.

The incarnations of embedded librarianship are many. The research is chock-full of so many different ways of embedding, though mainly concentrated on classroom and distance services. I would posit that librarians should not limit themselves to what may seem currently proscribed, but instead individualize the effort based on the amount of time you can reasonably invest, the department or class you wish to embed in or with, your relationship or buy-in with a particular faculty member, the subject matter, and so on. I truly believe that a one-size-fits-all model of embedding does not take into account all of the many factors that go into embedding and which I will go into in further detail in another chapter; namely, the role that most students and faculty members see librarians in (and usually that does not include the classroom) and our relationship with faculty who often, paradoxically, do not see us as "academic," though "skilled."

I offer this book as encouragement to begin the process. It is my hope that it is both theoretical and practical. As for me and my practice, I am primarily interested in actual classroom embedding and believe it to be true embedding, and so this book is dedicated to that *specific* practice. Other extremely well-written and informative books have covered virtual embedded librarianship and have done so well, but this book will remain, happily, in classroom territory.

It is my desire to provide a rationale, a way to get started, and to provide inspiration for an aspect of librarianship that is not only extremely satisfying, but also has the potential for making a huge difference. I hope this book can be a guide and a support to all librarians embarking on embedded practice.

RESOURCE

Drews, Kathy, and Nadine Hoffman. "Academic Embedded Librarianship: An Introduction." *Public Services Quarterly* 6 (2010): 75–82.

1
From the Beginning

Traditional Librarianship Takes a Different Path

Knowledge emerges only through invention and re-invention,
through the restless, impatient, continuing, hopeful inquiry human
beings pursue in the world, with the world, and with each other.

—Paulo Freire

TRADITION IN THE FIELD OF LIBRARIANSHIP HAS A STRONG hold in the collective consciousness. While most people not in the field could not give you specifics about what that tradition is as it relates to the field itself, they will be able to run off the list of stereotypes, still perpetuated to this day, much to the consternation and irritation of many librarians. Since we know that perception and language shape reality, we are often hesitant to innovate out of the (once comfortable, but now suffocating) box which skews what so many would think of as disturbing the comfortable version of librarians that most have: bun wearing, shushing, legs crossed at the (thick) ankles women, with a perpetual scowl—to say nothing of the many men in the field. But the good news is that when we begin to innovate, we can call the change into existence, and begin *doing*.

There is no end to the debates about the various and new roles that librarians seem willing and able to take up, particularly in academia. Are we professors? Are we simply capable of teaching a skill set not valued by most students and, sadly, by some academics? Has the Google age set us on the path of obscurity, along with our dusty books? Are we simply in the field as the curators of knowledge? Are we the smiling, cardigan-wearing support people in one-shot instruction classes?

I have had many discouraging conversations with otherwise very intelligent people about my chosen career, in which I have attempted to dispel the gross inaccuracies and, frankly, often insulting descriptions of the work that I not only do every day, but am wholly dedicated to. What I found is not surprising: people will believe what they want to believe no matter what you tell them, and so I simply just stopped talking. Not long after I became a librarian, just a few short years ago, I remember myself and two of my colleagues walking over to the dining hall at our university for lunch. The provost and one of the academic deans were walking on the path toward us. The provost and the dean both put up their hands like they were afraid of our approach toward them: "Oh no! Somebody let the librarians out! Run for cover!" We demurred a bit, embarrassed, maybe laughed half-heartedly so that we would not seem like "poor sports." They laughed themselves silly and so did a few stray students who overheard the little scene too. Well-respected and smart men, neither of them could know the effect their behavior, well-meaning as I like to believe that it was, would have on me that day. I was so proud to be a librarian—genuinely excited to have a career I could dedicate myself to, versus a job that would pay me while I marked time dreaming of something better. It was eye-opening to see (and other evidence would be consistently presented later) that perhaps others did not see me or my profession in the same way. This bears mentioning since I have felt and sometimes still feel that some of us may be held back by tradition—that innovation is good for someone else, but not for *us* in *our* profession, though evidence of dynamic change is evident everywhere in our field. We are hurt by the negative stereotypes that are perpetuated about us because, in essence, it misrepresents us as both people and professionals and prejudices us among the very people it is essential that we collaborate with and teach: faculty and students.

Every new implementation needs groundwork to be done, needs a clearing of the path. This can be difficult if the organization or library structure that you work within has fixed ideas about a librarian's role, most especially in the classroom. My colleagues and I, for instance, worked quietly and diligently for quite some time on various initiatives such as serving on more committees, giving presentations, diligently attending faculty meetings, making one-on-one connections with faculty both in our liaison areas, but also in a gesture of collegiality. In addition, we increased our reference outreach to students by encouraging more one-on-one consultations, which are now the majority of the reference outreach that we do. I mention this because making these subtle and not so subtle shifts both benefits the work that we do with our students and increases our professional profile on campus. In my experience, this is no small feat. The effort is definitely worth results. When I saw the need to embed in two of the classes in my liaison department, I felt that I was respected and situated academically in order to approach the head of the department as well as the two professors whose classes I wanted to embed in. I laid the groundwork and felt that, for the most part, although initially the professors did not have a very clear picture of what I wanted to do, how I would do it, and how it would benefit the students, they trusted me enough to agree. Then, of course, the real work began, but it started with a conversation and a plan. Things usually go better with a plan and I had one. But I was also cognizant of the fact that while going in with a plan, anything could happen. I decided I would be both flexible and reflective within and toward the process so that I was not only being as helpful as possible to the students in the class, but that I could assess myself in the process. Older or traditional faculty may *seem* agreeable, but may meet you with slight resistance, since they may not yet be able to see your place in the classroom, most particularly your place in *their* classroom.

Evan Farber, college librarian emeritus at Earlham College, did a considerable amount of work in the field of librarian and faculty relations—most specifically in the area of cooperation with teaching faculty. In his own words, he expressed what he believed would be the ideal: "where both the teacher's objectives and the librarian's objectives are not only achieved, but are mutually reinforcing—the teacher's objectives being those that help students attain a better understanding of the course's subject matter, and the librarian's objectives being those that enhance the students' ability to find and evaluate information."[1] In "A Report on Librarian-Faculty Relations from a Sociological Perspective" the authors assert that, owing to a variety of factors, there is an "asymmetrical disconnect" that keeps librarians and teaching faculty, for the most part, apart.[2] But, and this but is important, *only librarians view this disconnect as problematic.* This fact, in and of itself, is very telling—teaching faculty are where they need and want to be, while librarians aspire to a deeper role with and among faculty in order to fully realize the work that they do for the fuller benefit of the students. The authors go on to explain, as their research proved, that faculty really do not have a full understanding of what it is that librarians actually do, besides collection development and access to that collection. The authors stress that this does not seem to be a result of disrespect, but rather of perception, which influences the reason why faculty are not so eager for contact with librarians. Librarians, they say, perceive this disconnect through various factors such as a faculty member's protectiveness toward class time, and assumptions about lack of expertise in any given field (librarians are perhaps best known in the common consciousness as generalists, etc.). All of these factors not only influence access to the students (the common goal) but opportunities missed. There are many other factors that influence this disconnect which are beyond the scope of this book, but, suffice it to say, strides have been and continue to be made.

For many librarians it is a frustrating dynamic, this disconnect. So many of us know that if a teaching faculty member is not a regular library user, is not fully aware of the services both our brick-and-mortar buildings as well as ourselves as library professionals can offer, how can their (our) students know? The old adage that "relationships are everything" seems germane here. Those who would like to begin any initiative within our profession, particularly in academia, cannot discount the role and importance of relationships that begin with conversation, common ground, and a plan. Embedded librarianship is an invested experience and a time-consuming one, well worth the effort, but it is *highly collaborative* and will demand open and honest conversation between teaching faculty and librarians in order to not only map out logistics but to recognize and acknowledge each other's goals, separately, and then create goals together. Common goals are an absolute necessity, otherwise, not only will students perceive a disconnect, but faculty and librarian may begin to work at cross purposes—or worse, not be effective together in any meaningful way at all, which is just a waste of everyone's time.

William B. Badke, writing about the rigors of getting faculty to understand the importance of information literacy in the classroom (which is a salient argument for any collaboration with faculty), hits just the right nerve in his assertion that we need to be proactive in our approach and position ourselves in order to demonstrate to faculty our worth in both helping them with their research needs, in addition to, of course, their students:

> Beyond helping faculty learn how to navigate the complexities of new information tools, we are in a position to put ourselves forward as information experts who can help them with many aspects of their research. This may smack of a tactical maneuver but actually represents a genuine contribution that no one but information professionals can make. If the eyes of faculty are opened to what we can do for them, we have a much better chance of convincing them that their students need to benefit from our experience as well. We are, after all, affirming the very thing that faculty most value—their ability to serve their own discipline as well.[3]

STRATEGIES TO START WITH

- Strategize and socialize. Becoming recognizable and accessible to faculty on campus, as well as students, is good for the library, the students, your colleagues, faculty, and your mission.

- Look for opportunities to engage in both friendly and meaningful conversation with faculty.

- If you liaise with one or more departments, arrange, if you have not done so already, to attend at least one department meeting which will allow you to see how the group functions and to get an idea of what their preoccupations and concerns are.

- Prearrange time with the department chair to address faculty with your ideas about embedding.

- Keep it brief but well-structured, with room for collaboration and the teaching faculty's vision, as well.

- Be prepared to offer a rationalization for why such collaboration would be a good idea. Creating talking points and anticipating questions are good ideas.

- Don't feel the need to answer every question on the spot. Stop, consider your answer, and offer to get back to someone with an answer or an opportunity for further discussion.

- Keep notes on others' thoughts and ideas.

- Follow-up with an e-mail to those in attendance with the offer of further conversation.

FINAL THOUGHTS

All in all, I truly believe that librarians must *socialize* others, particularly in academia, to the true nature of our field including our education, our research interests, and our daily activities, not as a way of justifying ourselves, but as a way of showing teaching faculty our strengths and commonalities so that the groundwork can be laid for collaboration. We also need to be able and willing to assert our knowledge of best practices in our discipline in instruction sessions that can be more than just, for instance, the "one-shot" variety or the way they have always been done. As professionals, we have the agency to assert our views to faculty and present our ideas and proposals in the spirit of collaboration—and we should. It does not mean that we will always be rewarded for our efforts or be anointed on our heads for coming up with such good ideas, but professionalism dictates that we can say, for instance: "This doesn't work anymore, but this might. How about if we try?" The aforementioned strategies are offered as a wave of paving the road, and are especially designed for the individual librarian who has a vision that is fairly begging to be implemented, but who may be the first person in the department to do so. That was the position I was in. I learned a lot along the way.

Planning is essential, of course, but when you decide to be innovative, particularly with embedded librarianship, you may not end up in the same place you started out—we really do make our road by walking it, but that is the way it should be. Before you begin, you may want to lay some careful groundwork to increase the chances that your ideas will be met with enthusiasm and careful consideration. When librarians and faculty collaborate, all around, everyone wins.

NOTES

1. Evan Farber, "Faculty-Librarian Cooperation: A Personal Retrospective," *Reference Services Review* 27, no. 3 (1999): 229–34.
2. Lars Christiansen, Mindy Stombler, and Lyn Thaxton, "A Report on Librarian-Faculty Relations from a Sociological Perspective," *The Journal of Academic Librarianship* 30, no. 2 (2004): 116–21.
3. William B. Badke, "Can't Get No Respect: Helping Faculty to Understand the Educational Power of Information Literacy," *The Reference Librarian* 43, no. 89–90 (2005): 63–80.

2
Embedded Librarianship Defined

Necessity is the mother of invention.

—English proverb

LIBRARIANS HAVE ATTEMPTED TO DEFINE THE PRACTICE OF embedded librarianship for quite some time now. In fact, the genesis of embedding academic librarians began in branch libraries, where librarians would help to curate the small collections held by faculty members, which were eventually folded into larger libraries, which then became "branches." One of the main tenets of embedded librarianship, collaboration, goes back as far as the nineteenth century.[1] So precedence, of sorts, has been set. In theory it would seem that the definition would be the easy part; however, it isn't. There are countless variations wherever embedded librarianship is being practiced and to be sure, the practice is still growing, evolving, changing, and adapting. But I still have not defined it, have I?

The term *embedded* is one that most people will know from the news media begun at the commencement of Desert Storm, in which news media traveled with military units in order to report from the front lines. Embedded was a perfect way to describe the practice: up close and personal, in and among the fray. *There. Involved.* Throughout the history of the profession, in one way or another, librarians have often been embedded, but the term was not used until recently.

Because the focus of this book is exclusively classroom embedding, I can say that in this context, and context is important, to be embedded means to be situated within and among those whom one is serving. It is that simple. One-shot instruction, obviously, is not embedding. Partial embedding is a sort of paradox, but it is done. There is no substitute for not being in the classroom when one "embeds." When working closely with faculty (collaboration) and with students (teaching), it is essential to both share their space and contribute and participate in the classroom.

THE CLASSROOM AS LABORATORY

The word is out—actually, it has been out for quite some time now. The days of one-shot instruction just don't work anymore. I found this out early on and the literature increasingly seems to support this notion. I became all too aware of the wrong timing of the one-shot, became too conscious of my "one chance" to reach students, and became discouraged at the enormity of the task in comparison to the miniscule amount of time I had to achieve it. In addition, I felt that I was somehow "performing" instead of teaching, always with the thought in the back of my mind that this was my chance. Professors seemed to think that they had done their duty—done right by their students by having a librarian come to class to do "their thing," whatever, in fact, that "thing" happened to be. I was often asked to come to do a session in any given class even before assignments had been given! The students would stare at me, alternately nod off, particularly in early morning classes, or update their statuses on Facebook while I spoke. I knew the names of none of them and felt, nearly always, that I gave them nothing they would remember, and worse, nothing that I would have the opportunity to build upon.

Embedded librarianship provided an antidote for what I felt to be an increasingly difficult task. If we see the classroom as a laboratory, and we should, we can begin to clearly see the possibilities of what we can accomplish when we are placed there among the very students we aim to serve. Imagine being able to teach and assist an entire class of students who get to know you, and vice versa, as opposed to those who *may* make their way, by chance, to the reference desk, often at the eleventh hour, for assistance. The difference is stark.

Janet Swan Hill makes the point in her infamous article "Wearing Our Own Clothes: Librarians as Faculty."[2] She writes that the practice of librarianship is applied—that it is an "applied" field. She goes on to say that its laboratory is "the library itself." I would add (and she would certainly disagree) that by extension, so is the classroom, especially in these days of redefining ourselves within the profession. Things that happen on the edge are exciting—the unique position that librarians have in the classroom sets the stage for innovation, deep involvement, cooperation, collaboration, and assessment. This is difficult, if not impossible, to do in the limited and often random interactions we have not only with students, but with faculty as well.

To extend and further define the meaning of being embedded, one must think in terms of involvement. The librarian who chooses to be embedded becomes involved in the culture in which the class is situated. That may mean that if you are embedded in an English Thesis class as I am, you are making an effort to get to know not just the professor with whom you will be working, but by extension those within the department. You may go to events that they sponsor. You may negotiate office space or an informal sort of outpost within their department. You get the idea. Being embedded does not begin nor end with your actual presence in the classroom, but instead is a more inclusive approach to reaching your target audience, in this case, students, and providing them with instruction, support, and ongoing research instruction throughout the semester and beyond.

CHARACTERISTICS OF EMBEDDED LIBRARIANSHIP

- Developing, building, and maintaining relationships, which is a direct path to a true partnership;

- Delivering services in a way that answers the users' needs in a timely and personalized way with continuity;

- Maintaining a presence in and among the targeted user group;

- Learning, understanding, operating, and providing service within the space of the user; and

- Becoming acquainted with the discipline in which you are embedded.

FINAL THOUGHTS

All in all, there are any number of definitions of embedded librarianship in the literature, including those that are virtual. There are variables dependent upon context, budget, faculty relationships, size of institution, and any other number of factors, though the one constant is a real and abiding commitment to a presence with full participation and follow-through. In this expanded and deepened role, librarians serve as true collaborators with faculty in the learning and research life cycle, based on a proactive and revitalized model of librarianship.

But more importantly, librarians are able to reach, build, and maintain relationships with students, which is crucial to all of student learning.

NOTES

1. Kathy Drewes and Nadine Hoffman, "Academic Embedded Librarianship: An Introduction," *Public Services Quarterly* 6, no. 2–3 (2010): 75–82.
2. Janet Swan Hill, "Wearing Our Own Clothes: Librarians as Faculty," *The Journal of Academic Librarianship* 20, no. 2 (May 1994): 71–76.

RESOURCE

Norelli, Barbara P. "Embedded Librarianship, Inside Out." *Public Services Quarterly* 6, no. 2–3 (2010): 69–74.

3
The Importance of Being There

Presence is more than just being there.

—Malcom Forbes

ADMITTEDLY, THERE ARE A MYRIAD OF WAYS TO EMBED A librarian and many more ways to actually *be* embedded; that is to say, once you are "there," what you will focus on and how you will make your presence known are both highly individual and contextual. While I recognize the many, many shapes that embedded librarianship takes, I am primarily interested in "being there"—in proximity, which will be the focus of this book. In my own personal experience, embedded at a distance, that is, online, did not interest me as much as actually being in the classroom with the students I was there to help. My own personal bias and my own sense of how I could make a difference was clearly situated in the classroom. Moreover, I had a vision of how things would work in the classroom—how I would interact with the professor and the students, how important I imagined it would be to actually hear what they were hearing, watch them process themselves and each other, and use that as a springboard for my own involvement.

My own reasons for wanting to embed were very closely related to my interest in one of the liaison departments, English. I was a new librarian, eager at the reference desk, and in about mid-October began receiving some rather frantic reference questions regarding an English thesis. The questions varied in length and intensity, but a fair amount were from students simply throwing their hands up in the air, lamenting that they simply did not know where to begin. My own response was a bit of exasperation—how to help a student with the pinnacle of papers? Tougher, even, was trying to get them to calmly explain to me what the actual requirements were, and so on. A few handed me their assignment papers that were, I was told later, kept deliberately vague in order to allow for their own "vision" to develop. What was missing in the picture is what they were actually hearing in the classroom and how they were processing the information. I had no window, really, into that information. At the end of the semester, I made an appointment with the thesis professor, who met with me willingly but offered little comfort as he could not understand, "quite frankly, where the difficulty is coming from." Then he said, "They ask no questions in class. And I assume they know how to find sources—they've come this far and after all, they have been writing papers for four years now!" *Ah, the misconception.* I was expecting it somewhat, but not as much as was expressed. But the good news is, it gave me a starting point, and I began thinking and planning. I did not know much about embedded librarianship at that point, as none of my colleagues were "embedded" in the "traditional" sense, though our sciences librarian was the closest, doing more sessions in and out of the classroom than any of us. My instincts, coupled with the fact that my colleagues and I were looking for better ways to collaborate with faculty, told me that getting into the next semester's thesis class was probably a really good idea. However, I needed buy-in from the thesis professor.

I set up another meeting with him, but he just kept asking me what I could possibly do in the classroom that I could not do with the students in my office, one-on-one or during my hours at the reference desk. I admit to being flustered at his questioning. His eyebrows raised, he waited for an answer. I remember spreading all ten of my fingers out in front of me and placing them on my lap—because I thought that I had articulated my reasons as best as I could, already. He declined my offer of embedding (a term that puzzled him) and suggested that it might help students (and assuage me) if he required that each student meet with me, at least once, for a one-on-one meeting. I was frustrated, but I agreed.

It helped. Quite simply, being able to just sit and talk with a student in a mutually agreed upon time, without the kind of frantic desperation that we experienced the previous semester, made a world of difference. Because we know that learning happens in conversation, I felt that what was happening in my office, at my table (never while I am behind a desk!), was good and worthwhile. I asked each student to fill out an "intake" form, which collected various answers to questions such as which primary text they thought they would use, their comfort (or discomfort) with both databases and approaching librarians, and other pertinent questions. Each time they met with me I would keep notes on our meeting and have "action steps" for them. My other requirements were that the meeting would last no more than twenty minutes (they were encouraged to make another appointment), they should do more of the talking than I would, and they would be both encouraged and expected to take notes.

While they were only required to meet with me once a semester, imagine my pleasure at meeting many (though not all) students two or three times, at their own initiation. It was during these meetings that I was able to consistently reinforce the fact that research is a process, and that it is rarely, if ever, as easy as we want it to be. Moreover, the research process is not a linear one. I came to be very, very invested in the process with these students. I felt their frustration at the writing/research process and worked assiduously with them. The missing piece of the puzzle, for me, was that I really did not know what they were doing in class—each of them had their own subjective experience, but I approached each of them with a sort of veil of "unknowing." I wanted to be with them, in class—I wanted to be able to hear what they were hearing from the professor and I wanted to be able to see how and if they were processing things. While I had all sorts of ideas of how I would build my approach with the students in the class, how I could do this by implementing strategies and information literacy with the professor into the syllabus, I decided to work within the constraints imposed on me and then assess with the professor at the end of the semester.

I learned quite a bit through the process. While I had pressed this professor hard to be embedded, the truth is, it had most definitely served my process of working with students and my understanding of the commitment that embedded librarianship takes to have eased into it—by having a semester of working with the students with an eye toward further commitment the next time around. It became a process for me, much in the same way I have preached to my students about their research process: it takes time, and mistakes will be made.

At the end of the semester, I met again with the professor, who proclaimed that he saw an overall improvement in the quality of the papers that were turned in. He said that he was also consulted much, much less than he had been in all of the previous years of teaching the course. This pleased me, even though of course it was anecdotal. It was satisfying, nonetheless. Still, the goal was actually being in the classroom. I saw the need and was determined to make it happen. If it is true that we make our way by walking it, this is exactly what I set out to do. And I managed to achieve this goal when in the following fall semester, a professor with whom I had worked quite successfully in the past would teach the thesis course. He was enthusiastic about my participation; in fact, he welcomed it. I was on my way.

STRATEGIES FOR THE CLASSROOM

- Have a plan. While my instincts told me that being embedded in the English senior thesis course was a great idea, I needed to not only have a solid rationalization and plan on paper, but I needed to be able to articulate it in the clearest way possible.

- Set goals both for yourself and your students. How will you be effective in the classroom? What will you expect of the students? How will "being there" actually make a difference?

- Understand the realities of being embedded in the classroom; time is not the only commitment you will need to make.

- Clearly articulate your role during the first class. Most students do not think of librarians as professors in any way—in fact, they often have no idea what we actually do or what our education level is. Let them know! Introduce yourself. Explain yourself. Share who you are with the students you will be spending an entire semester with.

- Show up. While this seems incredibly and embarrassingly obvious, you must be consistent. To be sure, there will be days where you feel just like the students might feel—that you simply cannot drag yourself to class. Don't give in. Being there means just that.

- Do not melt into the woodwork. I will admit that I was so excited when I finally got my chance to actually be present in the classroom that I tried to be as unobtrusive as possible. This simply did not make sense—I was there to do a job! I led class discussions and I participated in them, too. I gave feedback on presentations. I made my presence both known and understood.

- Do not be afraid to make suggestions to the professor in class. I worked with a professor that I had known for quite some time and whom I greatly respected. There were occasions when he would remark to me during a class break that students seemed "low energy," or "disconnected." I would give a gentle assessment and often suggest a change of pace, some group work or other strategies that might change the tone of the class.

FINAL THOUGHTS

I will admit that I came to embedded librarianship the way I come to most things: largely by instinct and by what I felt and still feel has the potential for being a better way to do things. I have come to realize how important the actual desire to "be there" is in the entire process, because, to be sure, being embedded in the classroom can be arduous, challenging, and extremely time-consuming. Being there means being fully present and understanding that at times you will be sitting and listening and absorbing and other times you will be actively engaged. Being there helps you to gauge the confidence and frustration level of students. You will pick up on their boredom, their fatigue. You will see how their enthusiasm will wax and wane during different parts of the semester and on any given day. You will feel their desperation, feel their anxiety. You will come to understand how this will affect their performance in class, with assignments, with writing papers. You will find that you are not an objective person in the classroom—something I believe is a fallacy—because, really, who can escape their own point of view? You will have opinions, strategies, thoughts, and sometimes objections. And while you may not be the professor in the class, let there be no doubt that your task at hand is just as important.

One of the most important aspects of being embedded in the classroom is being in the privileged position of being able to observe the learning and research cycle of students *as it happens*, and to be able to fully participate and influence this cycle, rather than just enter it at irregular intervals, by chance, over the reference desk. Kesselman and Watstein put it succinctly when they assert, in their wonderful article "Creating Opportunities: Embedded Librarians," "If we are truly to be where the user is and to be user-centric, we need to be embedded. Embedded librarianship is a major focus for the future of our profession."[1] Additionally, and ultimately, being embedded exemplifies collaboration at its very best: "because the librarian becomes a member of the customer community rather than a service provider standing apart."[2] Of course, I could not agree more.

NOTES

1. Martin A. Kesselman and Sarah Barbara Watstein, "Creating Opportunities: Embedded Librarians," *Journal of Library Administration* 49 (2009): 383–400.
2. David Shumaker and Mary Talley, "Models of Embedded Librarianship: A Research Summary," *Information Outlook* 14, no. 1 (2010): 27–35.

4
The Importance of Relationship Building

If we are together nothing is impossible.
If we are divided all will fail.

—Winston Churchill

IN THE PREVIOUS CHAPTER I TOUCHED UPON THE IMPORTANCE of relationships. "Relationships," as the director of our library will almost daily remind me, "are everything." I have both witnessed and experienced the power of relationships to transform experience, nurture collaboration, and then sustain those collaborative efforts. As librarians, we have traditionally "played in our own backyard," not particularly feeling as though we were wanted (or needed) anywhere but the building we were housed in—ready and waiting when and if we were called upon for our expertise.

Much has been written about the different worlds in which librarians and faculty reside, with both librarians and teaching faculty weighing in on the divide. Traditionally, faculty have not seen librarians as equals, and have, in fact, seen them strictly in the sense of being in a position to offer "support," if they gave any thought to what their actual role happened to be in the first place. Librarians have often felt themselves to be in a subordinate and submissive position, figuratively, not only speaking when spoken to, but harboring both secret frustrations and desires for more recognition and more expanded roles, particularly involving collaboration and teaching. One of the problems seems to have been, and indeed, in some sectors, still is, that faculty do not seem to perceive a problem with their professional relationships with librarians. In fact, it has been observed that not only do faculty not perceive serious issues of any kind with librarians, but as well, they feel no particular deficit in this lack of connection.[1] But librarians have a different perception. And this perception can often stand in the way of initiating collaboration with teaching faculty. It is essential for embedded librarians to have good relationships with faculty for their initiatives to be successful. This, however, is often easier said than done. How can we, as librarians, begin to take the necessary steps toward good relationships with our faculty given our shared, albeit separate, history?

A bit of background into the traditional relationship of librarians and faculty may shed light on how best to navigate new territory. It helps to identify and understand the philosophical underpinnings that have been the barriers to collaboration. While any academic librarian could quite conceivably fill volumes with anecdotes of perceived slights and blatant, if not necessarily intentional, "dissing" at the hands of faculty, I remember one incident in my own career that, for weeks, made me feel as though I might consider a career change. I had been in my office when a faculty member called. She was in a building just a few yards from the library. She was having trouble printing and was going to "pitch a real fit" if someone didn't help her. She needed me. *Now.* I told her that as soon as I had a work study student available, I would send one over. She persisted in saying that she needed immediate help and asked me what was preventing me from coming over at that very instant. I should have known better, but my anger felt overwhelming, and so did my embarrassment. The incident, in my mind, seemed to mock not only all of the hard work that I and my colleagues were continuously engaged in, but also the many initiatives we were consistently putting forth that attempted to include faculty. We had been trying hard to dispel the notion that we just sat around waiting for something to do, waiting for someone to *serve.* In fact, that is exactly what it *looked* like, as faculty, when they did come into the library, would always glance over at the reference desk and find one of us there. We were seen as passive. Helpful, perhaps, but passive. In my own mind it was a bit of a turning point, and though I fully understood the stereotype we labored under, I found it hard to accept. There are misconceptions and mistaken perceptions galore.

Melanie Boyd, academic liaison librarian for collaborations in teaching and research at the University of Guelph Library, identifies two main perceptions, held by librarians and faculty members alike, that serve as a barrier to healthy working relationships and collaborations, and which can become further entrenched if librarians do not actively work to dispel them.

The first perception that Boyd points out is that librarians are not trained as teachers. Boyd is particularly astute in pointing out that neither are most faculty. I would also add that the library science degree is not seen as a particularly academic one, either. But Boyd points out that what we *do* share is "the challenge of translating a deep, unique area of knowledge and expertise to students—most often without the benefit of rigorous pedagogical training."

The second perception Boyd identifies is that of the librarian as service provider. She suggests "easing out of our lexicon as a defining characteristic that distinguishes us from faculty." Aptly, she points out why the notion of service is a perception: faculty provide service, too, as it applies to students. Librarians are often seen as in service to faculty (supporting their research, etc.), but the converse is simply not true. And because it is not true, there is an inequality in the minds of faculty.

And so identified is what I call the "great divide."

Librarians embedding themselves in the departments and collaborating in the classroom are ways in which that divide is bridged. And in fact, Boyd has a simple, what she calls a radical idea for enacting change. *Simply be where the faculty are.* Can we do that? Can we place ourselves among, with, and beside the faculty and, like the concept of an arranged marriage—the love, eventually, with patience and maturity, will come? Or do we work on building the relationship(s) first? This is an age-old "chicken and egg" dilemma perhaps.

A bit of both, perhaps?

In my own experience, I worked assiduously to make connections that would help to build relationships with the faculty in the English department, one of my liaison areas. My uneasy and tentative approach was no doubt instrumental in placing distance between the very people I sought desperately to reach, as well as affirming in their minds that I was perhaps no more valuable than what they were consistently asking me to do: order a specific journal, come to a class to "teach them how to do research" (usually when they themselves could not be there), or do any number of things that were, to be sure, the duty of a liaison, but in no way invited true collaboration. My voice was softer when I spoke to faculty; I looked down a lot. My credentials and theirs were uneven. These points are not small ones. I barely made a ripple in my attempts, at first, to build relationships with faculty, let alone the idea of pursuing something I desperately wanted to do: become embedded in the English senior thesis course.

When a new director was appointed at the library, she told us that our relationship with faculty would have to change, something we knew, but none of us knew exactly how. She herself was in possession of a doctorate and having held high-level administrative positions as well as faculty positions in her long career, she saw us for what we were: bright, determined, but scared. She'd both observed and witnessed our difficulties with faculty, including the fact that all five of us were unequal in our various attempts at relationship building with faculty. Some of us had met with (limited) success, and some with failure. None of us had yet to achieve what we all imagined to be a true collegial or collaborative relationship. She told us that perhaps the way in which we referred to ourselves might shift the faculty's perception a bit. At least, she felt, it couldn't hurt. She suggested that from that point on we would call ourselves *faculty* librarians, a term a few of my colleagues, if not totally against, were a bit confused by. One exclaimed, "That sounds like we *serve* faculty—not that we are on a par with them!" Still, our director, an extremely wise and strategic woman, insisted that we begin using the term—and that in her conversations with administrators and faculty alike on campus she would refer to us this way.

A word, indeed, shaped the faculty perception of our reality. We had bedrock, a firm place, from which to stand. And not in name only. We knew our value, but we also knew that others probably didn't—but now we had a name that placed us *among* faculty. In fact, we were already faculty (albeit, at the time, for purposes of governance only) but were barely, if ever, recognized as such.

This seemingly small step was a personal turning point for me. That place from which to stand felt firm underneath my feet and I was determined to go ahead, sometimes wincing, as much as I hate to admit it, and just work on my liaison department, one person at a time. The old stories librarians have been telling ourselves for so long, the old stereotypes we never tire of railing against and all of the righteous indignation, though I would never deny there is not a reason for it, felt stagnant. I needed, in fact we all needed, a new paradigm.

A NEW PARADIGM

Kempke suggests operating from a position of strength and confidence. Using Sun Tzu's *The Art of War* as his guide, he advises librarians to be intentional and targeted:

> My advice is to find a niche, to infiltrate a soft spot in the battlement—
> one that provides the best area to devote resources and is the most
> likely theater for success. Whatever post you station, communicate its
> importance and defend it aggressively. Identify the right leaders to fol-
> low or befriend. Target those in your way.[2]

While some may roll their eyes or wonder at his metaphor—war—it would be good to remember that some still believe that collaboration, indeed, relationship building with faculty is akin to going into battle. Badke, for instance, would rather see a librarian's time and energy better spent in the development of our own instruction sessions per discipline, rather than have to waste time on building relationships and attempting to collaborate with faculty. He goes as far as to say that "effective collaboration is not the norm."[3] I, and no doubt many others would agree, but surely cultures change, and even though faculty culture is seemingly stubborn, it too can change.

In my own experience, building relationships with my liaison area faculty was difficult and stressful. I knew that if I was going to make inroads into the goals I had for my work with the department in particular and with faculty in general, it was necessary for me to simply forge ahead. Strategies aside (of which there are many and which I will provide some of here), there is no substitute for simply beginning the process—and it is a process, to be sure with the knowledge that every effort will not cause a magical transformation in the perceptions that have probably prevented the relationships to begin with, but maybe more like two steps forward, one step back.

And remember that it is a process, imbued with all of the various pitfalls that prevent that forward and continuous line of progress. I say this not as discouragement, but rather as a realistic caveat—otherwise, one could wrongly perceive failure.

A NEW WAY OF BEING

Students definitely benefit from faculty-librarian friendships and collaboration in the classroom based on mutual trust and respect. Librarians and faculty who align educational goals and assess their impact on students are true collaborators. But the opposite scenario is bad for everyone. We have all seen the impact of the professor who is disengaged when the librarian is in the room. The students are confused as to why the librarian is there and why the professor is not delivering the content. If the librarian is not introduced and no context given as to why the librarian is standing in front of a class that the librarian would hesitantly, if ever, call his or her students, then the librarian begins at an immediate deficit. I have had professors look up from the laptops in the corner of a computer lab every so often while I was teaching when I asked them for clarification. Quickly, they would get back to what they were doing. Students witness this. Often, faculty members that engage in this kind of behavior are ones that usually do not know how to use the library at all—and so instead of reinforcing what I am teaching (always a great way for a session or sessions to go) they will leave it to the person standing in front of the room. Librarians then become the "experts" when they, the faculty want us to be—when it is simply convenient for them. When a professor asks me to come to a class, I have learned to first make sure that the professor is going to attend as well.

I have learned to suggest we reschedule the class for a time when the faculty member can be there. This is not always received well, mainly because we are often a "plug-in"—a way to still hold class even if the faculty member has planned to be somewhere else that day. When this has happened in the past, I have experienced great difficulty in engaging students on any level at all. The very appearance of a faculty member in class can help to support the teaching of the librarian, but when the professor was not in the classroom, many of my past sessions turned out to be empty and sad exercises in futility. And students are always wiser. Unfortunately, or fortunately, professors will often call or e-mail me a week or so later to ask me how the session went. They often demand attendance from their students, deeming it a "real" class, but the students deem it otherwise.

Let me use the above example to exemplify the fact that we really do teach others how to treat us. When I made a conscious decision that I was not going to be a convenient step-in for an absent professor, my colleagues were irritated. One of the first comments I heard was, "We just can't dictate which classes we will go to and under which conditions!" And what I thought was, that is *exactly* what we must do! We are professionals, after all. And spending an hour or more trying to instruct students who in many cases have no assignment to apply the skills to, and who know that if they really do need help they will just ask someone at the library for help, we can, with all honesty, say that such "interactions" are not worth our professional time—and most certainly do not benefit the students in any real way.

For relationships of any kind to work, it helps if there is common ground, mutual respect, and honesty. I began to think to myself that if I wanted faculty to see me as an equal, what was I doing individually as a librarian, and how were my colleagues and I functioning as a group of librarians that was an impediment to faculty perceiving us as their equals?

For one thing, faculty, who are notorious for not having any extra time whatsoever, particularly during a semester, would scarcely, if ever, deem it worthy of their professional time to do what they often ask us to do: wing it in a classroom of virtually unknown students, with no assignments to attach our lesson to and no "muscle" behind the expectations we have of students. Furthermore, and as another example, faculty are used to seeing librarians sitting at a reference desk, passively, just waiting (and waiting and waiting) for someone to help. Faculty members go home on the weekends and in the evenings if they can. They are not sitting around "just in case."

In light of these examples, I feel it is imperative to assert ourselves professionally, not only placing ourselves among faculty, but more importantly *enacting* a shift in the culture by realizing that we have standards in our own profession and we are not simply in service to faculty requests without filtering and assessing them through the lens of our own profession. It actually behooves us to do so. When I finally began making alternative suggestions for sessions that were scheduled too soon in the semester or before an actual assignment had been given, I spoke up—from a position of strength with research to back me up. I did not deny the request per se (though I might have if it were insisted upon against my better judgment) but instead made suggestions for another (better) way, by different timing. In more than just a few cases, this led to collaboration by default which, as natural progression would dictate, paved the way for more real collaboration, collaboration that was more intentional rather than a by-product of my simply being wary of what I was asked to do.

When faculty use the library they are more likely to recommend the library and its services to students. Some faculty, it would seem, are averse to the library. In my own library, I do not often see faculty members looking for their own books or doing their own research—many, if not all, have grad-uate assistants to do the work for them. I will often encourage faculty to use the library space as an antidote to their busy floors, to the ringing phones in their offices, or just for a new place to work that can offer a fresh perspective on whatever it is they are working on. It gets them into our space and has the potential for gradually becoming their space, as well. And it puts *them* in proximity to *us*. One of the ways that faculty can begin to know a bit about the culture of our profession is to spend some time in the spaces in which we reside. This is no small point. One can hardly build a relationship when we do not meet one another in a common space.

STRATEGIES FOR BUILDING RELATIONSHIPS

- Operate from a position of strength. Our expertise is needed but may not be recognized in the way in which we would like it to be. We are in service to both faculty and students, but forget the definition of *service* as a form of servility. Full faculty, too, are in the service of students. And we create a platform for better relationships when we can bring our expertise to the table and be able to talk about the possibilities in the classroom as collaborative partners. It is human nature to be attracted to those with confidence and self-assuredness.

- Become integrated on campus. This cannot be stressed enough. Opportunities for relationships are everywhere on a college campus. How you are thought of will go far in the endorsement of your value. And your participatory profile on campus should be high—it is an investment in the culture of the campus of which you are a part and affords you the opportunity to meet up with students in non-threatening and potentially fun activities outside of class.

- Speak often and well of your colleagues to others. While building personal relationships with campus faculty and others, do not forget to tout the achievements of your colleagues as well. This serves two purposes: it helps to spread their good reputations, therefore paving the way for better and more frequent collaborations for them as well, and it is also the collegial thing to do.

- Don't forget to close the circle and then open a new one. Circle back after encounters with other faculty. A simple e-mail stating how nice lunch was and a suggestion that time be made to do it again goes a long way. If you say you will get back with information, make it a priority! It will be appreciated and will inspire confidence.

- Realize that the chemistry may not always be there, but it should not stop you from trying. I have found some fellow faculty members extremely demanding, or difficult to work with in general. I used to feel hurt, offended, but came to the very liberating conclusion that I could build a satisfying work relationship with someone as difficult as possible and letting it go just that far was fine. Pushing a social sort of camaraderie with someone who is resistant probably isn't wise. Relax. It may happen over time. And if it doesn't, keep it professional!

FINAL THOUGHTS

All in all, the way we relate to others says a lot about who we are and very little about the other person. Personally, I look at how someone treats others as an indication of how they might treat me. Respect goes a long way in relationship building. You do not always have to like someone (and in many cases, you won't), but professional and human conventions dictate that whether you do or don't you still owe that person respect. So much so, that an onlooker would never be able to tell whether a particular person is friend or foe.

NOTES

1. Lars Christiansen, Mindy Stombler, and Lyn Thaxton, "A Report on Librarian-Faculty Relations from a Sociological Perspective," *The Journal of Academic Librarianship* 30, no. 2 (2004): 116–21.
2. Ken Kempke, "The Art of War for Librarians: Academic Culture, Curriculum Reform and Wisdom from Sun Tzu," *portal: Libraries and the Academy* 2, no. 4 (2002): 529–51.
3. William B. Badke, "Can't Get No Respect: Helping Faculty to Understand the Educational Power of Information Literacy," *The Reference Librarian* 43, no. 89–90 (2005): 63–80.

5
Clarifying Your Role in the Embedded Classroom

Appearance blinds, whereas words reveal.

—Oscar Wilde

ONE LEARNS FROM ONE'S MISTAKES, AND I HAVE LEARNED more than my share in the embedded classroom. Early on, I thought it sufficient and if I am telling the truth, quite advantageous for the students that I, as an embedded librarian, was present in the classroom. I felt rather empowered by my role as purveyor of information literacy strategies and had rather grandiose ideas about the "bridge" I imagined I would build between the students and the professor in the class. In essence, I saw my role as the "missing piece," the one that would help to pull it all together in the classroom. After all, how could having a librarian in the class not favorably amplify a student's experience of learning and his or her attitude toward what a librarian has to offer? I left out a crucial step. In fact, the first time that I was fully embedded in a classroom, I just showed up.

I took my seat at the long conference table and saw fifteen senior English majors. I looked around and smiled at everyone. The students smiled back. Some smiles were wider than others. Then eyes began to shift back and forth. I saw an amused shrug that one student directed to another. The professor came into the room and launched into an overview of the syllabus. Unbelievably, during that first class, neither of us had explained why I was there. The students knew who I was, and I knew them. In fact, because I am the English liaison librarian, I had encountered each of these students before in other classes, in one-on-one appointments, and over the reference desk. So why did it all feel so uncomfortable? For the simple reason that my role on that first day of class was never clarified. The students, quite frankly, simply had no idea what I was doing in the classroom. They could not see how my presence in an actual class would help them—if indeed they even thought that far. They were simply mystified.

The old adage sagely offering the fact that we teach other people how to treat us is quite apt here. Clarify your role in the embedded classroom early and often. Since such careful preparation with the professor in the class takes place long before you actually set foot in the classroom, most aspects of your collaboration including instructional design, special assignments, computer lab time, and so on, will be sorted out, and should be communicated to the students both on the syllabus and with a formal introduction. This is the best way to contextualize the librarian's role so that students know what to expect. The librarian is a co-collaborator, but not necessarily the co-teacher—a fact that if not stated will conflate the roles, leading to miscommunications all around. For instance, because of my and the professor's lack of clarification, I had more than a few students come to me to discuss the professor's comments on their drafts; they wanted explanations, verifications, and validations that I could not give—I did not grade the papers! While referring students back to their professor, I caused a lot of frustration among students who felt that I was in the position to help, but for whatever reason, didn't. Not a good way to begin. And what is not established early on is difficult or nearly impossible to establish later on. Clarifying your role, in large part, will affect the overall environment of the classroom. Ivey[1] has identified four behaviors that lead to successful collaboration in the classroom: a shared and understood goal; mutual respect, tolerance, and trust; competence at hand by each of the partners; and last but not least, ongoing communication. This collaboration is at the same time a clarification of your role.

Clarifying your involvement in the class (students will be frankly baffled by the term *embedded*) will help you to manage your role in relationship to the student support you will be delivering. McLeod, Fisher, and Hoover identify important key elements of classroom management that include the use of time and space, instructional strategies, and the importance of building effective relationships with students.[2] All of these factors influence the librarian's impact on student learning.

STRATEGIES FOR CLARIFYING YOUR ROLE

- Your name, title, office hours, office phone, and e-mail address should be placed on the syllabus.

- Both a written and verbal introduction on your role in class should be given.

- Expectations of what students can reasonably expect from your presence in class should be clearly stated.

- The limitations of your role should also be stated. If you will not be grading papers, for instance, it would be fair for students to know that ahead of time in order to avoid the scenario described above.

- Reinforce the collaborative nature of your role in class, while maintaining the uniqueness of your position and your added value to the students' experience.

FINAL THOUGHTS

The educational reformer John Dewey recognized the importance of the environment in the classroom (and to a great extent we influence that environment) by stating, "We never educate directly, but indirectly by means of environment."[3] When students know exactly why the librarian is in the classroom and what role, exactly, she or he will play, we create a climate that is conducive to learning, with no surprises and no hidden agendas.

NOTES

1. Ruth Ivey, "Information Literacy: How Do Librarians and Academics Work in Partnership to Deliver Effective Learning Programs?" *Australian Academic and Research Libraries* 34, no. 2 (2003).
2. Joyce McLeod, Jan Fisher, and Ginny Hoover, *The Key Elements of Classroom Management: Managing Time and Space, Student Behavior, and Instructional Strategies* (Alexandria, VA: Association for Supervision and Curriculum Development, 2003).
3. John Dewey, "The Project Gutenberg Ebook of Democracy and Education" (2008), retrieved from www.gutenberg.org/files/852/852-h/852-h.htm.

RESOURCES

Julien, Heidi, and Jen L. Pecoskie. "Librarians' Experiences of the Teaching Role: Grounded in Campus Relationships." *Library & Information Science Research* 31, no. 3 (2009): 149–54.

Manuel, Kate, Susan Beck, and Molly Molloy. "An Ethnographic Study of Attitudes Influencing Collaboration in Library Instruction." *The Reference Librarian* 43, nos. 89–90 (2005): 139–61.

Nalani Meulemans, Yvonne, and Allison Carr. "Not at Your Service: Building Genuine Faculty-Librarian Partnerships." *Reference Services Review* 41, no. 1 (2013): 80–90.

Stanger, Keith "Implementing Information Literacy in Higher Education: A Perspective on the Roles of Librarians and Disciplinary Faculty." *LIBRES: Library and Information Science Research Journal* 19, no. 1 (2009): 1–6.

Zmuda, Allison, Violet H. Harada, and Grant P. Wiggins. *Librarians as Learning Specialists: Meeting the Learning Imperative for the 21st Century*. Westport, CT: Libraries Unlimited, 2008.

6
Establishing a Teaching Style in the Classroom

More important than the curriculum is the question of teaching and the spirit in which the teaching is given.

—Bertrand Russell

M Y COLLEAGUES AND I HAVE SPENT A LOT OF TIME OVER THE years in meetings together discussing information literacy and all that it encompasses, but most particularly how it impacts our classroom teaching. There has been an evolution of practice, to be sure, in that amount of time as we have consistently reflected on our collective and individual practice. We have grappled with standardization, best practices, one-shot instruction, and the seeming lack of interest or attention from students and their professors for our efforts. There is an endless debate over the role of librarians in the classroom as well as the recent controversy over the necessity of information literacy. The times are changing, for sure, and while I don't normally mind getting caught up in the controversy, I have come to the conclusion that the endless debates that those in our profession engage in effectively displaces our attention from our current practice and our own agency. Instead, we need to think about how we can make a difference in our sessions, one class at a time. One hardly needs a mandate in order to reflect on our own practice and to simply try something different. Trust our own instincts? Well, yes.

I have an abiding belief that learning begins in conversation. My instincts and my own experience in the classroom tell me that when you engage a student in conversation about their "topic" you are often engaging them in a way that gives voice to an idea that has just been rolling around in their heads, one they may be really struggling with and not even know how to approach.

For this very reason, and the fact that I am often met with that glazed-over look by the students who I stand before, I have decided to take a "hands-off" approach during my first session with students in any given class. What this means is that the students before me and all of their attendant informational needs are, at that moment, more important than the technological tools and databases before them. In fact, I prefer to have my first (usually of three) session with students in a regular classroom and not a lab for this very reason. That means I get to look them in the eye, and they, too, get to size me up. They cannot hide behind a computer screen and I cannot use my "bag of tricks" to deflect the "conversation," where I believe the seed of real learning takes root.

Conversation is natural; so natural in fact, that most of us engage in it countless times over the course of a day in many different settings and we often do not think twice about it. Humans engage in conversation with one another as a way to share secrets, intimacy, an exchange of information, among other reasons. As a professor librarian, I have tried many different ways of connecting with students in the classroom—some successful, some failures. But one way that I have consistently been able to engage students and have them actually respond to my efforts has been to take a "hands-off" approach to teaching. This means that I decide to focus on conceptual teaching rather than teaching that is tool-based. This is a very intentional style of teaching on my part, and I can say with full honesty that it has worked very well in my classes and has been encouraged by the professors that I have worked with in the classroom, even when it has been very different from their own style.

I firmly, in the tradition of the great radical educator Paulo Freire,[1] reject the "banking" system of education—the notion that we, the educators, stand up in front of a room and "deposit" knowledge into the heads of our students who come to us as "blank slates" with nothing to offer and everything to gain—that is, what we as the "all-knowing" professor can give them. I want to do exactly the opposite. I want to break down those barriers and engage students in what they may be thinking. I will often begin with a conversation about the expectations they may have for the session—which are usually pretty low—I joke about how tired they look, how much coffee I myself just slugged down, how I know how difficult it is to go from a topic to a paper. I empathize. I meet them where they are. They begin to open up. But more importantly than getting them to speak to *me* in class, is getting them to speak with each other. I encourage a loud class. I like to pair them up and hear their conversations. I almost never have to remind them to keep on topic since it is a great relief to be given "permission" to voice their thoughts and concerns about the assignment at hand. Here are students, for a time, "unplugged," and it is both a rare and beautiful thing to behold.

Be prepared that this style of teaching may make professors nervous because it does not seem as though any "progress" is being made. *What about databases? Key word and Boolean searches?* I assure them that I take a scaffolding approach and that I will get to all of that and that the first session is just "priming the pump," for lack of a better term. Ideally, I get to speak to professors about this beforehand. I am a professional and I feel that it behooves me to act like one when I am in the classroom—particularly as an embedded librarian. This sometimes means that what a professor would *like* me to do is not actually the best way to approach things. Then we have a *conversation*.

Educational theories are continuously changing to reflect the time and place in which we and our students find ourselves. *This is a good thing.* Encouraging our students to begin to converse with themselves, with us, and with each other is far from radical, though in the present climate of tools-based learning, where content knowledge is packed into databases just waiting to be unlocked with a magical key, it can seem as though it is.

All of learning begins with inquiry; of this there can be no doubt. J. F. Lyotard,[2] the French philosopher, sociologist, and literary theorist, asks the questions all educators should ask themselves: "Who transmits learning? What is transmitted? To whom? Through which medium?" Librarians, in thinking about their approaches to information literacy, may want to begin with what seems most natural: getting in touch with your students and surveying the landscape of their thoughts. Allow for progress to be made through *process*. Begin by creating a climate that encourages the verbalization and articulation of their thoughts, fears, and their intellectual anxieties.

Kenneth Bruffee[3] has written extensively about the importance of conversation in education and learning. Bruffee has astutely stated, "Conversation is of such vital importance to learning that without it, few of us would stand a chance." Conversation forges community, and in a community learning and support of learning happens. It's a beautiful thing! A lovely by-product, too, is that while engaging students in conversation, you are laying the groundwork for a connection to be made. It almost always follows that if a student can make a connection with you in class, he or she will be more likely to seek you or a colleague out in the library, having begun a conversation with one of you outside of it. We can't underestimate the anxiety students seem to feel around librarians in the first place, so breaking the ice will serve our students well in the long run. And, after all, it really is about them.

Creating a conversational style in the embedded classroom goes a long way toward contributing to a dialogic environment rather than a monovocal one, something I will talk about in a later chapter. It is more of a democratic environment that encourages the voicing of opinions and questions and allows a student to hear his or her own "voice" in an environment of support and acceptance. I have found this to be one of the most rewarding aspects of being an embedded librarian: I have a bit more latitude in what I do to be able to draw out students in important ways. I have also found that students did not fear that I would be censorious with them or criticize concepts that they could not grasp at first. Because so much of what I do in the classroom is teaching students to conceptualize, they often have to vocalize their thoughts, let their words reverberate, and then have others join in the conversation. This is how thoughts and ideas become challenged, but also clarified and validated.

You know the old adage, "I don't know what I think until I hear myself say it"? It's true. It really is. And the librarian in the embedded classroom is in the ideal position to enact this process.

STRATEGIES ESTABLISHING YOUR TEACHING STYLE

- Students often have anxiety about libraries and are intimidated by librarians. Establish contact early and often with students. Setting up initial appointments with each of them where you discuss, among other things, what concerns they may have with the material in class and how you may help them specifically is a good place to start.

- Have students fill out an "intake" form which will collect information from them that will help you to establish a "baseline" idea of what their strengths and difficulties are with research. Take notes throughout the semester on this form each time you meet with a student. For instance, each time a student meets with me individually (which is often) I pull out their sheet and note any changes (for example, perhaps they changed the text with which they will be doing their thesis on), but I also am careful to note the nature of our conversation: the student's concerns, any insights, strategies shown, and so on. This approach is, admittedly, a bit ethnographic, but seems wholly appropriate and helpful, given our position in the class. No class is a monolith, and while the class may have certain aspects in common (they all need to write a thesis, they are all majoring in the same discipline, etc.) such as a knowledge base, individually their strengths and weaknesses and interests will vary greatly. Being able to understand where they are individually helps to enact and encourage cohesive learning together in the classroom.

- Set aside time after each class or shortly thereafter to "debrief" with the professor in class. In my case, both of the professors that I worked with were often surprised at their students' perspectives on what they were learning and the difficulties they were having.

At least in my case, there was a tendency to tell the professor that all was well when, in my individual sessions, they would admit that they were not. It seemed easier for students to be able to share that with me. I was seen as an ally in the class, a role that I acknowledge but am, of course, not limited to. Being able to debrief after the class while impressions were fresh helped to build upon, together, our strategies for the next session. Armed with what was working and what wasn't, we worked together to address the issues for the next and subsequent classes.

- Keep good notes. Keeping a process journal is a great meta-cognitive activity and a wonderful reflection tool. While we are often exhorting or requiring our students to keep a class journal, I have found keeping one indispensable. While some may think already being embedded in class is holistic, reflection on the process makes it even more so. Looking over your notes after class will help you to concretize your thoughts about your impact on student learning and other facets of the process. The process of keeping notes in general wholly focuses your attention as you are participating in the process.

FINAL THOUGHTS

While there are so many variables in the embedded classroom, preparing the students for your involvement is just as important as the preparation that you will do with the professor beforehand. Students need to know what they can reasonably expect from the librarian in the classroom . Whatever you decide, be consistent in your teaching style—if you begin fully engaged, by all means, remain that way. If you are the type to hang back a bit and decide that being participatory in class is not your best style, honor that. Be who you are every-where, but most especially in the embedded classroom.

NOTES

1. Paulo Freire, *Pedagogy of the Oppressed*, trans. M. Ramos (New York: Continuum, 2002).
2. Jean Lyotard, Keith Crome, and James Williams, *The Lyotard Reader and Guide* (New York: Columbia University Press, 2006).
3. Kenneth Bruffee, *Collaborative Learning: Higher Education, Interdependence and the Authority of Knowledge* (Baltimore: Johns Hopkins University Press, 1983).

RESOURCES

Julien, Heidi, and Jen L. Pecoskie. "Librarians' Experiences of the Teaching Role: Grounded in Campus Relationships." *Library & Information Science Research* 31, no. 3 (2009): 149–54.

Manuel, Kate, Susan E. Beck, and Molly Molloy. "An Ethnographic Study of Attitudes Influencing Collaboration in Library Instruction." *The Reference Librarian* 43, nos. 89–90 (2005): 139–61.

Nalani Meulemans, Yvonne, and Allison Carr. "Not at Your Service: Building Genuine Faculty-Librarian Partnerships." *Reference Services Review* 41, no. 1 (2013): 80–90.

Stanger, Keith "Implementing Information Literacy in Higher Education: A Perspective on the Roles of Librarians and Disciplinary Faculty." *LIBRE: Library and Information Science Research Journal* 19, no. 1 (2009): 1–6.

Zmuda, Allison, Violet H. Harada, and Grant P. Wiggins. *Librarians as Learning Specialists: Meeting the Learning Imperative for the 21st Century*. Westport, CT: Libraries Unlimited, 2008.

7
Classroom Embedding Creates Communities of Practice and Possibilities

Writing and learning and thinking are the same process.

—William Zissner

EMBEDDED LIBRARIANSHIP MADE SENSE TO ME EVEN BEFORE I had an actual name for the practice; indeed, before I knew that it was a concept of growing popularity. This was a good thing, in my case, because I was free from any strictures of practice that I felt I was transgressing. Instead, I began the practice of "being there" simply because I felt that I needed to be there. I had been feeling, with ever-increasing frequency, disconnected and auxiliary to the teaching process, and both witnessed and felt the sense of inertia and resistance so many academic librarians have felt from the students whom they are tasked to teach. I had no sense of the "ecosystem" of the class in which I showed up, was totally in the dark about their knowledge of doing research, what they had done in the past, and where the most difficulty often lay. And in a 45-minute session, I was never going to find out. I began having a lot of one-on-one sessions in my office, which both I and the faculty that I most often worked with would recommend. Here, students would ask me questions about things I had covered in class, vaguely remembering search strategies and other skills, but having totally forgotten them in the interim. At first I saw this as an abject failure on my part. Why couldn't I seem to generate any interest in research or search strategies in the information literacy sessions I was teaching? How did the majority of students ever hand in successful papers with relevant and authoritative sources? How best could I teach them in the limited time and frequency with them that I had? The answer came to me almost immediately. The truth was, I simply couldn't. What I felt would make my teaching effective and facilitate learning among students who did not deem library skills on any level to be important would be to be in the class with the students and to work collaboratively with the faculty member *in concert*, rather than at cross-purposes.

COMMUNITIES OF PRACTICE

While attempting to forge my way into more embedded practice, both literally and figuratively, I learned a lot from Jean Lave's and Etienne Wenger's model of learning in what they call a "community of practice." Simply, this means that learning occurs in the same place in which it is applied. While some might argue that this practice does not strictly apply to the classrooms in which librarians may embed themselves, I assert that it does—and, in fact, in my own experience, has worked to my, the professors', and the students' great advantage.

To be sure, the practice of embedded librarianship will not fit all of the strict characteristics of the practice, but I felt that the three main tenets of this theory of learning made a lot of sense to me and validated the way in which I felt my presence could make a difference. The basic tenets[1] of the practice as defined by Wenger are as follows:

What it is about: understanding the community as a *joint enterprise,* the foundation of which can be and usually is renegotiated by those who participate in it;

How it functions: members working together to a common purpose which enhances a feeling of connectedness and builds community; and

What capability it has produced: a shared repertoire of communal resources by way of routines, sensibilities, artifacts, vocabulary, styles, and so on.

What I understood from this theory of learning was that learning happens best in a community where goals are shared, proper support can be given, and knowledge is not deposited, but rather created through a variety of participation strategies. Wenger makes an important distinction when engaging in this practice: that this community is different than a community of interest or one that is situated in a common geographical place. This is an intentional community and, even though in the case that I will present, that of being embedded in a English senior thesis course, some would argue that it is a required community, it is a community nonetheless and one which I could define by the dimensions of the practice listed above.

In the embedded classroom the librarian's job is no longer "decontextualized," a problem that I would assume many academic librarians feel as we are "kept in our place" by making what I have often thought of as "appearances" in class. In these "appearances" we are asked to teach *skills* (which faculty have never failed to point out is a much lower level than actual knowledge, which is prized), with usually only the bare outline of the assignment that students are given, if even that. We have not been able to understand classroom lessons from the students' vantage point, simply because we have never been in class with them. Traditionally, we have been situated to deliver content or "skills" (often seen as rather low level) at times that were not particularly useful in terms of learning. Before there was an embedded librarian working in thesis class, students would occasionally ask for my help over the reference desk, but I felt it was all rather sterile. The thorough reference interview revealed that far from knowing how to do research for such an important class, it was assumed they already knew how to do the research, and often when they finally came to me they were frustrated, and by that point merely wanted me to find the sources they were looking for, rather than take them through any steps. This is what I have termed the "find me something and let me plug it in" reference question. For a class that relies so heavily on research, the students really had no sense of what to make of their own topics, where to go to find correct sources, but more importantly, they had no idea how to *think* about their topics. And this last point, for me, as it pertains to embedded practice, is one of the most important. Being in the classroom and building a learning community while you are there entails, for the most part, being "conceptual" rather than tool-based—at least in the beginning. Moreover, learning becomes focused in interactions and relationships, meaning that the librarian is uniquely situated to be able to aid in initiating, facilitating, and maintaining these types of conversations. While I recognize that the situation that I am writing about here is not strictly egalitarian—the professor leads the class and the librarian mediates a lot of the understanding and the learning that takes place in the spaces in between—a community does, in fact, take place and pleasingly, sooner rather than later. Learning begins to take shape in community as students are encouraged to think out loud, have their ideas critically and respectfully questioned, and are encouraged to fine-tune or change their perspectives on an issue based on conversations and diverse viewpoints in the learning community. Students begin to hear what they are thinking, and their thoughts are released and added to and expanded upon. The student finds a way to express him or herself, slowly gaining confidence in him or herself and the information process. Lave and Wenger praise this style of learning in contrast with internalized learning because "increasing participation in communities of practice concerns the whole person acting in the world."[2] Wastawy, Uth,[3] and Stewart believe that the "social nature of information seeking means that essentially all information seeking can be seen as collaborative at some level."

My experience in the embedded classroom exemplified this point almost perfectly. I and the professors in the two sections I participated in saw early on the fear in students' eyes at the word *thesis*. Indeed, this was their thesis class, their capstone, a chance to choose a text that resonated with them on some level and write critically about it, to be presented at the end of the spring semester in front of English faculty, adoring parents, friends, and peers. A seemingly tall order to students, but to the rest of us a natural culmination of four years of learning. In regard to students, I have learned from my mistakes and I no longer make any sudden moves, but rather simply observe. In the first few weeks of the fall semester, I began to see a group dynamic doing its job, and while the professors and I had rather methodically set up and integrated my exact role and the strategies I would enact as the librarian in the classroom, none of us knew, exactly, how the class would function as a group, as the learning community that I had envisioned. While each and every student was known to us—having encountered each of them in class over the years—how they would help or hinder one another (yes, it happens!) was an unknown. Admittedly, I as the librarian had more leeway in being able to observe and take notes on both social and academic behavior in the class. I also watched to see which, if any, alliances were being forged, so as to "exploit" those alliances for the greater good later on. One of my aims was that the class would, indeed, function as a community of learners, or as we like to say at my university, a "community of scholars." I was enacting what Annemaree Lloyd would call an "outside observer"[4] position, an ethnographic stance in which to situate myself in order to be able to understand the class dynamics along with their informational needs. Lloyd's work is based on her fieldwork observing firefighters, leading her to understand that "information literacy in a workplace context requires recognition that information and knowledge are socially produced and distributed, and that access to it can be affected by social relationships."[5] This ethnographic approach comes easy to me, though some may bristle at the seemingly passive activity. All of the planning and setup done before an embedded class actually takes place becomes an exercise in futility if the group dynamic is not taken into consideration. And while one can hardly know the needs of a class or how it will function before everyone is assembled together in the same room for a few weeks, it is a necessary step in fulfilling the promise of the learning community. One can easily translate Lloyd's use of "workplace" to be "classroom," where she describes the setting of this sort to be made of "a constellation of skills, practices and processes that depend on relations with experts who afford and mediate the process and thereby, enhance the information practices of the novice."[6]

MEDIATING

Much of the way I see embedded librarianship being enacted in the classroom is that of being an intermediate between the students and the professor and facilitating instances of learning and knowledge acquisition. I usually tell my classes that among other functions, I will be there to get them from point A to point B and even further still. Sometimes the distance between two points is lesser and sometimes it is greater. This is largely dependent on a myriad of factors, though I feel it is part of my job to figure this out. This is a unique position to function from, as my students have not had this opportunity before. As much as I am touted by the professor in the class to be "our very own resident information specialist," I feel that I am certainly the bridge between the professor and the students. In class I take notes on everything from content to students' expressions and the questions that they ask in class. This helps to provide a "picture" of each session. I have been able to discuss with professors after class where I think there are areas of misunderstanding. These can be smoothed over and explicated in the next class. After a few weeks, I begin to address those issues in class. This is when some real work begins and I move (but do not abandon!) from my predominantly quiet ethnographic stance as observer into that of active participant and mediator. To more fully realize that role, it was my responsibility in one of the sections of the thesis course to initiate group discussion, pair up students as research partners, and solicit questions or raise a particular thorny topic in the literary theory that we read in class. Theory seems to confound students—coupled with the fact that they are learning some difficult concepts while at the same time attempting to apply some of them to the thesis they are writing—so the discussions usually go from abject frustration, for instance, "What does Derrida have to do with my topic anyway?" to a sort of totally breaking down an issue or topic and facilitating participation in putting it back together again. The average student struggling alone is less likely to do this. Usually frustration will win, and a sort of paralyzing effect will set in, preventing the student from moving from one point to another, preventing the advancement through the weeks that is expected of them. I have long taken a hands-off approach to teaching information literacy, preferring instead a conceptual approach, where I have long felt learning begins. When we begin with a conceptual approach, we allow for greater participation *among* students. We can see how knowledge is created, in community, not isolated, unchallenged, unspoken. Ideas come out of the dark into the light of day.

James Elmborg in "Critical Information Literacy: Implications for Instructional Practice" takes a community view of learning that encompasses both the social and political concerns of educators and theorists, among them, Freire and Giroux. This view moves away from learners as strictly individual, alone in the wilderness, needed to prove or perform knowledge, but instead shines a light on learning as produced, distributed, and used as, in essence, a socio-political process that depends upon and encourages the participation of community. He further asserts that "people produce, read, and interpret texts in communities not in isolation. Communities reach consensus about interpretation, sometimes easily and sometimes contentiously. Literacy cannot be described, therefore, in broad terms as a set of universal skills and abstractable processes. Rather, literacy is in constant flux and embedded in cultural situations, each situation nuanced and different from others."[7] Librarians have previously been focused on a skill set—a one-size-fits-all "tool" or a set of tools that can be applied to any information or research need. But conceptualization, the process of meaning-making, is missing from this formulaic approach and it has clearly outlived its usefulness. Since the librarian is instrumental in leading students to those information sources, it makes sense that the librarian, as well, takes part in the conceptualization process, and that process takes place in the classroom, among a community of learners, with the regularity (such as a semester) needed to build upon the process step by conceptual step.

TAKING THE LEAP

Perhaps some who read this will feel that what I propose is not concrete enough, is devoid of strict guiding principles, and does not have enough agency in the classroom given our current roles in academia. If you have gotten to the point in which you are embedded you have that agency. This approach does take time, and it does take stretching teaching muscles that may have, as yet, been unstretched. But at the outset, embedded librarianship itself is not business as usual. The practice entails a change of culture, a change of expectations, and a change in the way we enact our profession, our goals, in the classroom. It seems almost heretical to some librarians that we would have our own goals for what our (yes, *our*) students will learn in the classroom and how they will learn it. When we are embedded librarians, we can no longer be content (as if we ever were) to sit quietly on the sidelines. If, in fact, our expertise is needed (and it is), then we need to assert what we know in our own discipline and give a rationale for why it is used, why it is needed, and how it affects change in the classroom.

In the past I have been frustrated to the point of distraction when I am asked to teach something in a way that I know will in no way benefit a classroom of learners. What is worse is that such a lesson will often reinforce to students (and others) that our lessons are useless, boring, and not applicable *in the moment* to what they need. One of the reasons that I chose to concentrate only on embedded librarianship in the classroom is because I feel so strongly in the librarian as a full participant and facilitator in and among a community of learners, rather than simply being embedded in an online learning system, a strategy which has its place, but does so with technology and from a distance. I am a proponent of hearing, listening, engaging, and assessing from right where the students are. A messy process, to be sure, and one not suited for everyone in every situation.

LEARNING COMMUNITIES ARE CONSTRUCTED

Because learning communities are constructed, as in the example of my English senior thesis classes, students can benefit from the shared goals and shared language of the subject and topics at hand. At the very least, these students are bound emotionally and academically by one common goal: each of them must produce a thesis. What I have found after years of being embedded in this class is that nearly every person, at first, has no idea how, exactly, they can or will reach that final goal. That one big commonality binds them from the beginning. They know this at some level, but not on a conscious one. They have not allowed themselves to get to the point of what they themselves might produce, let alone how exactly it will get done. And most if not all are not worried about how anyone else is going to do it. They just know that they have to. It is at this stage that I along with the professor will work on group dynamics, linking students in research groups and encouraging interdependence on each other. Traditionally, in my experience, students do not like "group work" and so they will often misunderstand the intent of the research groups. They will not be constructing an assignment together, per se, but instead they will be grappling with concepts together. Because often everyone is at different levels of understanding on any given topic, this strategy helps them to help each other to understand and removes the authorities from the process. They learn to depend on each other. As the librarian, this is my cue to work on the periphery for a while, to do the ethnographic observing I spoke about earlier, to watch and try to learn their particular learning styles, their anxieties, how they function in their group, and, of course, what their special interest or capability is in a topic. Lave and Wenger speak of "legitimate" peripherally as being an empowering position, "as a place in which one moves toward more intensive participation."[8] But, they warn, this is not a position in which one should situate oneself as a distinct position per se. Neither is the "center," as they define it, an appropriate position to remain in. Even "complete participation," as they see it, suggests a closed-off domain of "knowledge or collective practice." They prefer the term *full participation* denoting that which does "justice to the diversity of relations involved in varying forms of community membership."[9]

I will often talk to students and their need to "grapple" with concepts that they do not understand. And the process is often confusing, messy, and frustrating. I urge them to often take leaps in their thinking, while telling them that the process itself will cost them nothing. (I have seen students struggling and studying alone, going through the motions of attempting to gain knowledge, or what they believe is an understanding about the subject at hand, but their efforts are often strangely decontextualized from any collaboration that could be taking place.) Librarians can integrate learning strategies that help students to grapple with intellectual concepts and problem solving by the creation, location, and evaluation of information *together*.

Librarians can help to implement various modes of conceptualization, learning styles, conversations, and explication of texts. This is done not necessarily separately from the instruction provided by the professor (though sometimes it may if this has been mutually agreed upon beforehand), but instead in concert and collaboration. It is not separate from learning in the class, but instead, integral to the learning needs of the class. Conceptualization of a topic, indeed, the very way we think and approach a topic often comes before we begin to have students place their fingers on the keyboard to begin what is an often frantic search for "articles" —not information per se, not specifically what they, in fact need, but *something. Anything.*

While topic learning in classrooms is expected of students, and is in fact seen as the goal, traditionally "library skills" have been thought of as "auxiliary" to the main subject knowledge of any given course. The word *skills* denotes lower-level learning. In the embedded classroom as a community of learning, librarians can integrate subject content with information literacy strategies so that they are not separate learning tracks, not unintegrated but holistic.

STUDENTS AS APPRENTICES

Our professional literature is filled with both anecdotal and statistical evidence that students, particularly millennials, do not know as much as they think they know. They are facile with being able to use technology, do Google searches and come up with something which they can (and often do) shoehorn into their research. Or, in fact, they can change their research topic entirely to somehow "fit" the information that they have, with great relief, found. How they are able to actually make sense of what they have found, and in fact even knowing in the first place what it is that they actually need, seems often not to figure into their information-seeking equations. There are a few reasons for that, as I have seen in my embedded practice. One is that they simply do not know what they do not know. I have lost count of how many times, as an unembedded librarian, I have been asked to do information literacy sessions only to meet the blank stares of students, some often visibly irritated. "We know this already," they will often tell me. When I ask them if they have any questions, rarely if ever do I get a response. They seem to think that with a myriad of databases, the free Web, and most especially Google, if they can't find it there, it simply does not exist.

The second reason is that I believe most students think that they should already know what they are in class to learn. They have not reconceptualized what they are tasked to do as "inquiry" which is deeper and wider than research, which seems to be a more "targeted" approach. How does a student begin to explore a topic in which they feel as though they must already know something? *With great difficulty.* Most students feel as though they are alone in their "unknowingness."

I would like to take Jean Lave's concept of the apprentice in a community of learning and use it as a metaphor to fit into the way in which I attempt to enact the concept in class. We start at the beginning.

STUDENT AS APPRENTICES
IN THE LEARNING COMMUNITY

Recognizing that students bring tacit knowing to the class and acknowledging that students who may feel deficient or intimidated by the scope of what they are required to accomplish in the class are beginners, apprentices help to contextualize expectations. Any student in any given subject can be seen as an apprentice simply based on the fact that they are taking a particular class. We will rarely if ever encounter students who consider themselves experts on any given topic.

Speaking to students about knowledge acquisition and their part in making that happen sets them up to be active rather than passive participants in their own learning. The librarian will facilitate collaboration and interaction between and among students with questions or problems that they will learn to grapple with together. It has been acknowledged that throughout the entirety of our lives we encounter more instances of collaborative learning than of individual learning.[10] I have seen that students know how to draw one another out in regard to expressing their thoughts or difficulties with the subject at hand. I have witnessed tongue-tied students in class attempting to express themselves, emboldened by an emphatic "Yes!" or a nod of a head in their direction, validating the students' response. The classroom becomes a laboratory of learning, not a place to showcase the knowledge one perceives oneself to have, but rather a place where ideas are often confronted, intellectually challenged, revised, expanded, and built upon.

When we grapple together with their topics, we are not yet using the "tools" that they are used to librarians beginning a lesson with. We deal in concepts first, because how we think about and conceptualize a subject will determine how and why we will use a particular tool, such as a database, and so on. I consistently remind my students that because our tools cannot think for us, we must conceptualize what we need before we begin to use one. We become *practitioners*, producers of our own knowing. Over the years I have had heated conversations about a conceptual approach with my colleagues and others in my profession. It would seem that "concepts" are relegated quite low, along with "skills," in preparing students to "know" what they need and want to know. Exploring concepts is a disposition of the apprentice as one learns by doing. Concepts are not meaningless abstractions, not showpieces of capricious thought, with no endgame, but are rather the result of great mental activity and when fostered in a classroom community can develop into useful strategies for knowing and into pathways to understanding. When facilitating the kind of classroom community that prizes a conceptual approach, the practicing in community of what we aim to know, we must be careful not to present these concepts as fixed or rigid, but instead ever-evolving and developing in class. The student as apprentice in the learning community must be allowed, in fact must be actively encouraged to contribute to and benefit from others in their learning community.

This approach is not always intuitive to students, and some may resist, given the propensity for education to still be, in many instances, a passive practice, of listening and note taking, of perhaps doing a group project with others that they may or may not have any sort of connection with at all, but basically learning, struggling, and processing on one's own. The embedded librarian can help to aid in the enculturation of this community by facilitating his or her own instruction at the outset to be one of open inquiry.

I have begun to dislike the term *research* as it applies in this situation, as it seems to leave out the curiosity aspect of finding out, the journey involved and not just the end result. I prefer the openness of inquiry, the way it "invites" the learner. Even with senior college students working on their final projects, I knew the word was an intimidating one and seemed to imply one way of doing things, and either you knew how to do research, or you didn't.

I would often begin sentences with the call to "explore," which was meant to encourage exploration together. I listened more than I spoke and I stayed with them through the process, but with varying levels of involvement. I was careful not to interfere too much when they would begin a line of inquiry and I allowed them to take it where it needed to go unless it got so off-topic that it became counterproductive. This did not happen often.

Because the class was involved in writing an English thesis with the authors and topics as varied as there were students in the class, the professor and I would start the class with a question for discussion, something that they'd discuss together while at the same time having their specific text in mind. One of us would write the question on the board and we would ask everyone to write it in their notebooks. We'd ask one volunteer to read it out loud. We tried to make the questions accessible in terms of discussion, but conceptual enough to encompass a variety of responses that students inevitably would explore with ever-increasingly open minds. Once such question was "Is there such a thing as universal experience?" It was interesting to see students cling vociferously to their own points of view in the first few classes of the semester as group dynamics began to take shape. By the fourth week, our "community" of learners had built trust and mutual respect and felt that for all intents and purposes, they really were in it together. And, I believe, better for it, each and every one of them.

STRATEGIES TO ENCOURAGE A COMMUNITY OF LEARNERS

- Have patience with group dynamics. Even if students know each other, the classroom is a unique setting—they do not yet know you as the librarian in the classroom, nor you and the professor in the classroom, nor all of you together. Some processes will occur organically.

- Encourage participation in class by showing a tolerance for differing opinions (no matter the subject matter of the course) and mistakes. Students will have different opinions and make mistakes. Class discussion can be modeled by the librarian and the professor by having discussions between and among each other and the class.

- Everything can be a teaching moment and often in indirect ways. Students can often find their way around a particular problem or difficult research dilemma by talking it through. Resisting the urge to jump in and solve problems will encourage students to grapple with issues to find a solution, thus empowering them further.

- Respect what students do not know. I have often been among librarians who endlessly and often bitterly decry what students do not know, which does not quite make sense—that is why they need us! The privileged and unique position of the embedded librarian provides numerous and often vivid insights into what students do not know—thus providing wonderful opportunities for learning. Be grateful for the insight, which is not often seen through chance encounters over the reference desk!

FINAL THOUGHTS

If we are good alone, we are better together. The embedded classroom is an incredibly unique opportunity to create and nurture a community of learners. Having patience with group dynamics, encouraging a warm, accepting, and non-judgmental environment will encourage the expression of thoughts and attitudes and will encourage students to do the work they are capable of doing. The embedded librarian can help to transform the classroom into a true laboratory of learning.

NOTES

1. Etienne Wenger, "Communities of Practice: Learning as a Social System" (1998), Systems Thinker, www.co-i-l.com/knowledge-garden/cop/lss.shtml.
2. Jean Lave and Etienne Wenger, *Situated Learning: Legitimate Peripheral Participation* (Cambridge, UK: Cambridge University Press, 1991).
3. Sohair F. Wastawy, Charles W. Uth, and Christopher Stewart, "Learning Communities: An Investigative Study into Their Impact on Library Services," *Science and Technology Libraries* 24 (2004): 327–74.
4. Benjamin R. Harris, "Communities as Necessity in Information Literacy Development: Challenging the Standards," *The Journal of Academic Librarianship* 34, no. 3 (2008): 248–55.
5. Annemaree Lloyd, "Information Literacy Landscapes: An Emerging Picture," *Journal of Documentation* 62, no. 5 (2006): 570–83.
6. Ibid., 576.
7. James Elmborg, "Critical Information Literacy: Implications for Instructional Practice," *The Journal of Academic Librarianship* 32, no. 2 (2006): 192–99.
8. Lave and Wenger, *Situated Learning*, 36.
9. Ibid.
10. Lauren B. Resnick, "Learning in School and Out," *Educational Researcher* 16, no. 9 (1988): 13–20.

RESOURCES

Arp, Lori, Beth S. Woodard, Joyce Lindstrom, and Diana D. Shonrock. "Faculty-Librarian Collaboration to Achieve Integration of Information Literacy." *Reference & User Services Quarterly* 46, no. 1 (2006): 18–23.

Brown, John Seely, Allan Collins, and Paul Duguid. "Situated Cognition and the Culture of Learning." *Educational Researcher* 18, no. 1 (1989): 32–42.

Fuller, Alison, Heather Hodkinson, Phil Hodkinson, and Lorna Unwin. "Learning as Peripheral Participation in Communities of Practice: A Reassessment of Key

Concepts in Workplace Learning." *British Educational Research Journal* 31, no. 1 (2005): 49–68.

Gabelnick, Faith. *Learning Communities: Creating Connections among Students, Faculty, and Disciplines: New Directions for Teaching and Learning.* San Francisco: Jossey-Bass, 1990.

Howard, Jeffrey P. F. "Academic Service Learning: A Counternormative Pedagogy." *New Directions for Teaching and Learning,* no. 73 (1998): 21–29.

Lave, Jean. *Understanding Practice: Perspectives on Activity and Context.* Cambridge, UK: Cambridge University Press, 1996.

Lave, Jean, and Etienne Wenger. *Situated Learning: Legitimate Peripheral Participation.* Cambridge, UK: Cambridge University Press, 1991.

Lennings, Oscar T., and Larry H. Ebbers. "The Powerful Potential of Learning Communities." *ASHE-ERIC Higher Education Report* 26 (1999).

Mitchell, Coral, and Larry Sackney. *Profound Improvement: Building Capacity for a Learning Community.* Philadelphia: Taylor & Francis, 2011.

Voelker, Tammy J. Eschedor. "The Library and My Learning Community." *Reference & User Services Quarterly* 46, no. 2 (2006): 72–80.

Westney, Lynn C. "Conspicuous by Their Absence: Academic Librarians in the Engaged University." *Reference & User Services Quarterly* 46, no. 3 (Spring 2006): 200–203.

Zhao, Chun-Mei, and George D. Kuh. "Adding Value: Learning Communities and Student Engagement." *Research in Higher Education* 45, no. 2 (2004): 115–38.

8
The Embedded Librarian as Facilitator of Process

The goal has to be right for us, and it has to be beneficial,
in order to ensure a beneficial process. But aside from that,
it's really the process that's important.

—Benjamin Hoff, *The Tao of Pooh*

I HAVE ALWAYS VALUED PROCESS OVER PRODUCT, AS THE OLD dictum urges us to do, but realize, of course, that in academia, we all must produce. That's life! I needed to think through a process that worked not only for myself, but for my students as well. Coming to a more conceptual approach, as I have touched on earlier, revealed to me that it is, perhaps, one of the best ways to enact learning in the embedded classroom, and an embedded librarian can be the ideal facilitator of that process.

Again, my frustration with doing most information literacy sessions was the fact that I was deprived of *witnessing*, and thus deprived of *understanding* exactly how students were learning. In fact, I was in the dark about what kind of process students were going through to reach their end goals. Or not. But more importantly, I was deprived of the opportunity to *reach* them and guide them through this process. This was a source of great frustration to me, because I know from years of working reference that it takes some time to figure out and understand what kind of help a student really needs versus what they actually ask for.

In the years before I actually became embedded, I would encounter students who simply wanted information, or sources, or *something* (usually peer-reviewed, although few knew what that meant) they could walk away with—verifiable proof that they had something, which meant that that something, the journal article or book, would help morph into the project that they were expected to hand in. But in my experience, few students knew what to actually do with that article, that book, that citation or abstract. I noticed that students rarely had difficulty finding something on their *topic*. That seemed to come easily to them, something they would often mention with pride, being "digital natives."

I have stood in front of many classrooms in which I encountered the same students I'd encountered in another class for another professor and they would roll their eyes at my presentation, my attempt at teaching them a thing or two. And yet, when I would poll the class on their information literacy skills, beyond being able to do simple searches in proprietary databases, few knew how to evaluate sources, how to fold research into their papers, evaluate authors for authority, or identify the experts writing in their discipline. Faculty often seemed oblivious to these shortcomings, and yet I was expected by them to do what I was increasingly beginning to believe was impossible—in the amount of time I had and with the infrequency with which I encountered students in the classroom. I had no time to process with them, nor they with me. I have a colleague who consistently repeats to his students in information literacy sessions that "research is never as easy as you'd like it to be." Knowing that can be half the battle, because I believe that most students have a mistaken idea of what research actually is to begin with.

KNOWING IT ALL BEFOREHAND?

We do ourselves and our (mainly) undergraduate students a disservice, in fact, by the continued use of the word *research*, which implies a concept that many undergraduates do not seem equal to. "Inquiry," conceptually, allows for the freedom (and reality) of not knowing, but puts one on the road to find out. Those of us who have already jumped through the many hoops of fire in order to earn our degrees cannot fully understand how daunting the research process is for students. So many of them seem to think they need to already know what they are looking for when they begin to look! I have had students apologize to me because they simply do not know what they are looking for. Others, sometimes prompted by their professors, begin the process with very fixed topics and not only do not allow themselves to fully crack open the topic to reveal the issue, but are frustrated when their inquiry process somehow leads them into different directions, as indeed it often does and should! But however many times I have communicated this to students both individually and in the classroom setting, any deviation from the fixed idea or topic or subject that they begin with distresses them, and in the end becomes counterproductive to their inquiry process. I have come to believe that it is easier to work with a student who has no idea where to begin. Of course, my experience comes from working with students in both English senior thesis as well as a required course for English majors, "Interpreting Literature," but the difficulty with research and inquiry spans nearly all of the disciplines.

The tendency for students to front-load their research process (I deliberately use the word *research* in instances where students attempt to merely find sources that will confirm their assertion of their topic) is one that I see more often than not. A few years ago, before I was fully embedded, I asked a senior student what the hardest part of research was for her thesis and she answered, with all seriousness, "Figuring out how to use all of the research I'd printed out and read." This student had so many difficulties in the completion of her thesis because she simply could not and would not deviate from the topic she chose very early in the semester, when evidence presented itself, early on, that her topic, in this case, gender roles in *The Great Gatsby*, could be looked at from more than just a few angles. As a result, her paper was poorly conceived and poorly executed and contributed nothing to the conversation or anything new to the body of knowledge about the topic. I took it as a personal failure as the librarian for the class that I could not really "reach" her or others like her.

IT BEGINS WITH THOUGHT

Christine Bruce[1] writes about the "relational" approach that those who teach can use when instructing students about information literacy, which focuses on the learners', "conceptions." To this end, Bruce formulated a theory, which is based on four specific features about learning and conception:

1. Learning is about changes in conception.
2. Learning always has a content as well as a process.
3. Learning is about relations between the learner and the subject matter.
4. Improving learning is about understanding the students' perspective.

These four points made so much sense to me, and in fact, was a validation of sorts because I had a sort of tacit knowing that these points speak to. It has been my experience both in and out of the embedded classroom and as I enact learning in any situation I am in as a librarian, that learning really is about changes in one's conception. Making students aware of their process (meta-cognition) will allow them to understand how they learn better. The professor in the class, while it goes without saying, is highly invested in actual learning; he or she is, by necessity focused more on content and often leaves the research/inquiry process to a librarian.

It is helpful to look at the six conceptions of information literacy that were the result of Bruce's study of educators at four universities in Australia, in the hopes of further providing a clearer understanding of information literacy:

1. information technology
2. information sources
3. information process
4. knowledge construction
5. knowledge extension
6. wisdom

The last feature on the list, frankly, took me by surprise. I rarely, if ever hear the word *wisdom* in relation to students or information literacy. "Wisdom" humanizes and elevates the process of research to one of inquiry in that it implies that students will gain so much more, in the end, than just a paper to show for their trouble. It implies that there is a higher goal than just the tangibles that we can measure. Bruce is careful, however, to make it clear that these conceptions of information literacy are not a prescription, not a one-size-fits-all for what is a highly personal and variable process that is dependent on many factors. Instead she asserts that any one person's experience of information literacy or learning is "intricately woven, revealing different patterns of meaning depending on the nature of the light cast upon it."[2] This was a liberating philosophy because it reinforced that for me, the one-size-fits-all approach of teaching information literacy, standards notwithstanding, was a wrong-headed approach, and those inclined toward an embedded approach would probably agree.

LAYING THE GROUNDWORK

While I work with two different professors for each thesis class, both have been supportive of my approach in the classroom. It took more than several meetings with the professors, beginning in the spring and lasting through the summer, for us to discuss and implement this approach. At first the professors were reluctant, thinking that what I wanted to do in the class would take too much time, as both of them are very content-driven, understandably. It was my job to constantly reiterate my value in the class. One would be naive to imagine that taking a member of the faculty's consent or permission to fully embed in a class meant that they fully understood what it is we are trying to do. In actuality, I believe few of them are even sure how or what we do during regular classroom instruction. It was my job to explain this as well as I could, which was frankly, difficult for me in the beginning. "Why" was the constant refrain, questioning that I continued to have to answer, and, quite frankly, felt that I had to justify.

One professor explained to me that her syllabus would be set up in a way that would take the students through the process of writing the thesis step-by-step, but when I took a look at it, what that really meant was that there were specific dates when assignments were due—such as pre- and subsequent drafts. The rest of the class focused on literary theory, in which they would include two approaches in their final papers. Providing dates for drafts, while a necessity to keep students on track, was not a *process,* but rather a *schedule.* My own feelings on being auxiliary to the learning process for so long were difficult to squelch, but I knew that if I was going to spend the time and energy to embed in this class, I was going to make a difference, or at least try my best to do so.

I asked the professor for time to look over the syllabus and to use my own teaching philosophy to more fully conceptualize how I could use her syllabus as a framework to embed information literacy practices and processes. She agreed. We met ten days later and I had more of a concrete plan and approach. Still, I sensed some resistance, which I then, as now, believe to be not only the proprietary attitude that professors have with both their subject matter and their classes, but the genuine doubt, not so much about a librarian's ability, but how that will play out in the classroom. Embedding, by its very nature, can be *planned,* but not *scripted.* In other words, one learns as one goes along, but it is better to set goals and methods that will encourage success, though of course, not guarantee it. I found this out the hard way, actually, when I just assumed that all of my careful planning, which played out so brilliantly in my head, was instead met in reality on several occasions with indifference, resentment, or bafflement in the class—and that by the students, to say nothing of the professor!

Managing my expectations was something that I eventually learned. It seemed like all of the advice that I'd preached to students over the years about process was the same advice that I forgot to apply to my own situation. I'd read several books and many articles on embedded librarianship that talked of an endless number of approaches including being embedded in a virtual sense, at a distance, in science, in the humanities, up, down, and all around, with careful steps, but nothing truly prepared me for the experience until I was actually doing it. No one would dream of being a virtuoso the first time they picked up a violin, so I did not understand why I thought I could take our students through a process that would be like a walk in the park. But it was a start.

THE RESEARCH BLOG

One of the strategies I envisioned for the class was a research blog that would be done each week, and would be embedded in our learning management system, Blackboard. Because I was driven by a conceptual approach to the students as a way of modeling process, the professor and I decided that each week I would post a question that would require the students to reflect on what was happening in class and their reactions to it. My thinking was that they would feel freer expounding upon the questions I would pose to them on their own time, and feel freer to answer in more meaningful and complete ways. While the professor preferred that I submit the blog questions or prompts to her in advance, I explained to her that I felt that this defeated the purpose. In fact, each week my question would be in response to activities or discussions in class, which not only made the exercise relevant, but also gave the students the valuable time involved in allowing something that was discussed in class to filter down and then reflect upon it more fully in the blog. Admittedly, while waiting for group dynamics to happen, the blog posts were rather short and to the point in the beginning. I felt that students were giving me answers that they thought I wanted to hear. Because I wanted and needed a baseline of information from students in the class, the questions I asked them to answer, first, turned out to be ideal pre-assessment questions, and, in fact, I used them as such:

- List, in steps, your research process.

- Describe your research process.

- What aspects of research do you feel fairly confident in? Please list and explain.

- Which databases are you most comfortable with and why?

- What would, in your opinion, be an unacceptable source for research and why?

- What kinds of resources have you used, predominantly, in your past research projects (e.g., books, databases, Wikipedia, newspapers, academic journals in hard copy, videos, Ted Talks, etc.)? In other words, what are your "go to" sources?

- Have you ever consulted a librarian for help with research without being required to do so?

- Are you comfortable approaching a librarian with research? Please explain.

- What would be an example, in your opinion, of the best type of research help you could receive?

- What has been unhelpful to you in the past?

- Please feel free to add any thoughts about the research process and your relationship to it.

I attempted to make the questions as open-ended as possible. While the responses varied, not a single student reported that they felt at all intimidated by approaching a librarian in the research process, though, not surprisingly, few reported that they ever felt the need to do just that. The students expressed an overwhelming sense of confidence in the research process, which did not surprise me. In my own experience, students tend to overestimate their ability to locate and evaluate sources and take a very distinct pride in being able to locate what it is they think that they need. But as I have stressed before: finding sources has never really been a problem.

Armed with the answers from the first blog post, I initiated conversation and gently challenged the class on some of their answers. For example, there was a distinct difference in the way they spoke about their own confidence in the process of what they called research and the difficulty many of them expressed in actually doing it. So, I wondered, which one is it? I felt compelled not to jump to my own conclusions which told me how mistaken they really were—that it was ego and age that led them to believe they knew, in every instance, what they were doing. Once we entered into conversation, slowly but surely what emerged was the fact that they really *did not know what they did not know*, though it was evident that they knew *something*—quite a bit, in fact, but they needed someone (librarian as mediator) to urge them along. To explain more clearly, they knew that there was a rupture somewhere along the line with the way they attempted research, but they simply did not know how to put together the pieces of their own understanding.

One student blurted out "Somehow, I know it's not about the databases, but I really don't know another way to begin." Once that was out, we could really begin. The student seemed to feel validated by the nods and murmurs of assent that were filling the room. These thoughts need to get airtime, need to see the light of day where they can be dealt with. Another student explained how she usually is reluctant, for any reason, to change direction in a research process even when armed with new knowledge or perspective. I have stated before that I knew this to be true, but hearing a student say it out loud again helped us work out as close as we possibly could exactly why that was true. This led us to talk about the fact that amassing "information," in fact, shoehorning information into your paper is not really research—or even inquiry for that matter.

The constructivist theory of learning has always greatly interested me and I could see that this theory of learning seemed apt to what was happening in this class. This theory puts forth two basic features: that we construct our own worlds based on our own experiences and perceptions and that "construction" entails the totality of a person, incorporating their "thinking, feeling and acting in a dynamic process of learning."[3] So while the students may have difficulty with concepts in the beginning, what we know is that we can tap into their thoughts and feelings, their tacit knowing, by beginning a conversation, which brings to light thoughts and ideas. In the thesis classes, I could clearly see how the students brought their entire selves into the process, most specifically since all of them had to choose a literary text to focus on and they often have very personal reasons for choosing a specific text. This text is almost always a piece of literature that resonates with them in very deep and specific ways, such as the student who wrote about Sylvia Plath's *The Bell Jar* because her sister was depressed to the point of suicide several times, or the student who chose *Ender's Game* by Orson Scott Card because she questioned her own place in the educational process, mainly because her foreign-born parents compelled her to go to college at a time when she wondered what she really wanted to do or how she could possibly succeed in a field she had no interest in. To look at these students and think that they brought nothing to the table was inherently wrong and would be denying the totality of who they were and what they were capable of.

In fact, the actual conversation that we had in the third class of the semester very much modeled the beginning of the inquiry process. And I pointed that out to them. "This," I said, "is how we begin the process: we talk and we think and we write, *before* we do anything else!"

Before the explosion of information, John Dewey,[4] writing in 1933, identified what he termed five phases of reflective experience, which exemplify the process by which an individual gathers and uses information to learn. Thinking, in fact, conceptualization, and then the awareness of the process is integral toward learning and gathering information:

Suggestion: a new idea, incomplete

Intellectualization: beginning to conceptualize the problem

Guiding idea: beginning to interpret

Reasoning: interpreting armed with facts and information

Action: idea tested

Dewey recognized the stages of doubt as integral to the gathering information stage, and in the beginning I could see the uncertainty clouding the faces of the students before me. When they are told that their uncertainty, that their *unknowing* is a natural and expected part of a complex problem, they can take a breath and move to the next step. Telling them what they can expect greatly alleviates so much of the anxiety that they feel in approaching any assignment.

To be able to further the process outside of class, I assigned students as research partners. The paired-up students would meet regularly outside of class and grapple not only with the assigned work in class (discussion theorists and writing about theory), but they would also go through the steps of their inquiry process with each other and keep notes on those meetings. Not surprisingly, it was much easier for one student to see faulty thinking or a wrong-headed approach in a process that was not their own. They articulated what they were thinking, where they were going with an idea, explained how they got there, and allowed themselves to be challenged and supported by one of their peers. We would discuss these meetings in class. I wanted them to be fully conscious of the process, because it was working and I wanted it to continue to work. Eventually they began to see how one idea gave birth to another and they identified leaps in higher-level thinking as it pertained to their topics, but more importantly, discussion in class and with their research partners turned *topics* into *issues*. I had to be explicit in explaining the difference: you start with a topic and with inquiry that topic turns into an issue to explore.

CONCEPT MAPPING AS A GATEWAY TO PROCESS

I have discussed with my colleagues the fact that I use concept mapping as often as I can. Some did not immediately see the value, while others were reluctant to have students do anything that even remotely resembled the handing out of a work sheet to be completed. "I can hear the groans now," one colleague said, tilting his chair back against the wall, rolling his eyes. As a rule, I don't like work sheets, and find that the students find them particularly off-putting when asked by a librarian to complete them—I know, I've tried it a few times.

The best strategies are the simplest when it comes to process. I hand out a very simple template of a circle connecting to other circles. In fact, the whole page is filled with circles and lines connecting them one to the other. I only ask that they put their predominant subject in the big circle in the middle. In my class this might be the text they are using for their thesis or the issue they are grappling with in the text. So to use the same example, my student, Dana, who was firm in her resolve to simply explore gender issues in *The Great Gatsby* was urged to fill out the concept map and begin to make connections. Afterward, they would sit with their research partners and go over their maps with one another, tracing lines of thought and subtracting, adding, or correcting some circles as a way to begin to firm up and concretize their thoughts. The class was always very loud when I had them converse with their research partners, and I and the professor in the class would walk around and both join in and monitor the conversations so that we made sure the students were staying focused. I collected the concept maps to better understand where students were in their thinking processes and then copied each one for myself and gave them back. I asked the students to hold on to them and to refer to them as needed, which a few admitted to, was often. In fact, many students had more than a few concept maps in which they could trace the stages of their conceptualization process. This made so many of them down the road feel like they could see *tangible* progress in their thinking, what I like to call "getting from point A to point B"—movement that they often find hard to conceive of in the beginning, but when nurtured and encouraged in a thoughtful way happens quite naturally. When students experience small successes in thinking and process, it clears the way for more of the same. Students begin to build their knowledge base both alone and together and begin to see (however slowly) how their work contributes to a body of knowledge. They see that this is, in fact, how knowledge is created, how we make our contributions to cultural production and is, in the end, so much more than just a project or a paper or even a thesis. The concept maps, the conceptual work in general led them to interrogate their own preconceived notions, and instead focused them on issues that would be possible to explore further. The work, the process, becomes a meaningful activity; a means to an end.

THE BURKEAN PARLOR

The Burkean Parlor,[5] put forth by Kenneth Burke as an apt metaphor for the way in which students enter into the conversation of research, exemplifies research as conversation, and is the ace in the hole for the embedded librarian:

> Imagine that you enter a parlor. You come late. When you arrive, others have long preceded you, and they are engaged in a heated discussion, a discussion too heated for them to pause and tell you exactly what it is about. In fact, the discussion had already begun long before any of them got there, so that no one present is qualified to retrace for you all the steps that had gone before. You listen for a while, until you decide that you have caught the tenor of the argument; then you put in your oar. Someone answers; you answer him; another comes to your defense; another aligns himself against you, to either the embarrassment or the gratification of your opponent, depending upon the quality of your ally's assistance. However, the discussion is interminable. The hour grows, late, you must depart. And you do depart, with the discussion still vigorously in progress.

Perhaps everything that I have written thus far can be summed up by reading the above passage as nearly the perfect metaphor for what I am attempting to enact in the embedded classroom. You will be able to see that I come back to conversation over and over again, because I believe it to be the very foundation of all that we do with students. Sharing the Burkean Parlor with students allows them to see, in theory, what it is like to enter into the conversation of research and inquiry, and how, despite what they may feel in the beginning, it is an incredibly natural process that we all engage in, particularly when we are not focused on it. Consider how students might share details of their lives over the lunch table in the dining hall. Students challenge one another, add to the conversation, create allies of understanding, and shift their viewpoints or alliances based on incoming information or the changing of particular details. This is a natural approach that should not be at all foreign to students; in fact, they will recognize themselves in this process. It is essential that they know something of the topic before entering into the conversation—something, anything—and then listen well, an aspect of conversation that many are not yet good at. Listening well will help them to critically evaluate and to interrogate the claims being made. And it is important for them to know that the conversation is ongoing—in fact, it may lay fallow at times but it is always going on. Whether or not you, as the embedded librarian, are facilitating discussion or the professor in the class is, this conversation will allow you to pick up on weak points in critical thinking or gaps in how students begin the process of inquiry. To join in any conversation, one must have a frame of reference, otherwise everyone is just talking at cross-purposes, simply to hear the sound of their own voices.

CAPTURING THE PROCESS

In my own process, I am usually scribbling away during these conversations noting the following:

Is everyone engaged in the conversation? It is common for certain students to always monopolize the conversation. Every class has a firebrand, someone who keeps things lively. I note who is doing most of the talking, who is asking questions, and who is on the fringe of the conversation or not participating at all. Usually these patterns will reveal themselves early on. Once you identify them, you can break the patterns that don't keep the conversation on point and moving forward. Moreover, you can encourage those who have not found their voice yet to participate by asking lead-in questions, bringing them off of the periphery. It makes the process more democratic and productive.

Are students bringing in sources or references to the conversation? While our in-class conversations will usually (but not exclusively) be based on assigned readings, it is interesting for me to note who students are bringing into the conversation—the expert(s) writing in the subject area, and so on. While not scientific by any means, this can be an indication that not only has a student paid careful attention to the readings, but the student is comfortable in sourcing them and referencing them for discussion. This is an important part of the process.

Are students getting "stuck"? Sometimes students will talk themselves into a corner and find it difficult to extricate themselves. This will often cause a break in the flow of conversation, though in and of itself, this is not necessarily a bad thing. I like to use the word *grapple*. A lot. If language shapes our conception of reality, by telling students that they will need to "grapple" with concepts this prepares them to do the "heavy lifting" that the inquiry process requires. I make note of this when it happens, because it reveals to me the way they are thinking about things. It is much better to get "stuck" in a class conversation, where someone is likely to pull you out, than at your computer, alone, your thoughts going around and around in circles.

Are students taking notes? I was very surprised when I began to take careful note of who was writing during class discussions—in fact, the majority of the students were. They were taking note of certain points, and in some cases, when I would randomly ask a student what he or she was writing down, the reply was that they were formulating their thoughts on something someone just said, and did not want to forget until they could enter the conversation. If you find that your students are not taking notes, it would be good to encourage them to do so. It will help them to see how thoughts and ideas take shape and give birth to better and more complex ideas.

My own note-taking process is one that I advocate any chance that I get. This process is highly reflective, in exactly the way the student process is. As an embedded librarian, so much of what we will try, in the beginning, may not work the way we thought it would. Taking notes during the process and reflecting on our practice later helps us, as co-educators, to better strategize in the classroom. For instance, one of the professors that I worked with liked to start the class with a critical question, something that tenuously reflected the theoretical readings that were assigned for each class (and which intimidated students to no end), but were broader in scope. The professor, a gregarious, though intellectually intense person, would pose the question and then ask students for their thoughts. One such question was: "Does the artist have a responsibility to the public to create morally and ethically responsible art?" For the first thirty or so seconds there was nothing but the sound of the proverbial crickets. Students shifted uncomfortably, hid behind their computer screens, and nervously coughed. Or shut down entirely. This exasperated the professor somewhat, but somehow, we managed to get through the first few minutes of what could barely be called a discussion. Then the class continued with instruction. A few days later, the professor said that she was concerned about the lack of participation in the class—how they seemed not to be able to orient themselves to the question.

Despite my own immediate impressions, my notes revealed a few things about what had taken place. Among other things, they were afraid to be wrong. I'd noticed the nervous gestures, the tentativeness. The more the professor prodded them for opinions or answers, the tenser the atmosphere became. This led me to the idea that she would let me know what the critical question she was going to ask was, and then I would fold that into the last few minutes of class talking about where and how they could find some background that would help them to contribute to the discussion. We conceptualized search terms together that would lead students to information they would need to parse, and that could help to enlighten them on the topic and ease their anxiety about jumping into a discussion that would now have some context.

The professor argued that while she had no real objections to what I wanted to do with the class, she felt that the theoretical readings, from which the question was formulated from, should suffice. I reasoned that maybe they should—but clearly, they weren't. She shrugged, and told me we could take a "let's wait and see" approach. This was the result of my attention to details in class, the notes that I took, and the post-reflection that became part of my practice as the embedded librarian in the classroom. This was another instance in which I could put forth information literacy strategies embedded in student process and model what really is inquiry.

Looking over my notes even now reveals several things to me, things that were successful and things that I probably would not do again. For all of its prescriptive advice on embedded practice in the professional literature, being an embedded librarian is a highly individualized process, not unlike the process each and every student embarks on in their quest for information. The librarian in the classroom is at a distinct advantage because we are able to both observe the class and the students (a luxury few faculty have) and be able to instruct, as well. And being able to truly facilitate that process is no small thing. In fact, it can and should be one of the cornerstones of what we do in the classroom.

STRATEGIES FOR FACILITATING PROCESS

- Begin with emphasizing that everything is a process; that the work for the class students are currently in is no exception.

- Equalize the process and the goal. I have, with anguish, watched students semester after semester make veritable grocery lists of the papers and assignments that need to be done (often at the last minute), and meanwhile that process, that wonderful concept that gets you to the finish line, is almost always obliterated. Implementing assignments similar to the ones in this chapter can take them through the process while still getting them to their goal. I like to say to students, "Yes, in the end you need to hand in a thesis, but the process is going to get you there." It can be painful or it can unfold over the allotted time.

- Teach students to manage their time as a way of managing process. For instance, endless times over the years I have had to break the bad news to a student that a book or an article that they have requested on the same day as their paper is due was not going to arrive in time. Not even close! My mantra to students has become: "The work is worth it. Honor it by building in enough time to do it right."

- Encourage mini-goals. For instance, in my thesis classes when we are in the early stages of information gathering (the easy part!), students often lose sight of the fact that they will then need to evaluate that stack of articles. Help them to set a deadline. Students have pushed against that approach by telling me, quite dramatically, that they simply don't have time until _____ (fill in the blank). I ask them to choose two articles, find forty-five minutes in the day (doable!), annotate, underline, highlight, and sum up. Then I ask them to meet with me to discuss. Forty-five minutes is doable. Soon, they are doing it on their own.

FINAL THOUGHTS

Everyone who is reading this book will have their own experience of process, or the steps taken toward an end goal. In fact, nothing can be completed without it. Some will argue that long before librarians were "embedded" in classrooms, students got along just fine. And that may be true. But the acceptance of librarians in academia (often as faculty) has moved into the mainstream, and the importance of information literacy is widely recognized not only as needed, but essential in a world teeming with information. The librarian in the classroom finally emerges as co-collaborator along with faculty, and then some.

Integrating information literacy skills in the embedded classroom directly affects and influences student processes, so that student learning in general and the research/inquiry process in particular is not the trial-and-error method used by a large majority of students, but one that is interventionist, inspired, directed, shared, and reflected upon. It is less stressful for students, too!

NOTES

1. Christine Susan Bruce, "Information Literacy Education," in *The Seven Faces of Information Literacy Education* (Blackwood, Australia: Auslib, 1997), 42–62.
2. Ibid., 174.
3. Carol C. Kuhlthau and M. J. Bates, *Seeking Meaning: A Process Approach to Library and Information Services* (Norwood, NJ: Ablex, 1993), 15.
4. John Dewey, *How We Think* (Lexington, MA: DC Heath, 1933), 12.
5. Kenneth Burke, *The Philosophy of Literary Form: Studies in Symbolic Action* (Baton Rouge, LA: Louisiana State University Press, 1941).

RESOURCES

Anderson, Karen, and Frances A. May. "Does the Method of Instruction Matter? An Experimental Examination of Information Literacy Instruction in the Online, Blended, and Face-to-Face Classrooms." *The Journal of Academic Librarianship* 36, no. 6 (2010): 495–500.

Campbell, Kathy. "When a Librarian Enters the Classroom: My Experiences Teaching a Freshman Experience Class." *College & Research Libraries News* 69, no. 10 (2008): 606–17.

Dweck, Carol S. "Motivational Processes Affecting Learning." *American Psychologist* 41, no. 10 (1986): 1040.

Gokhale, Anuradha A. "Collaborative Learning Enhances Critical Thinking." *Journal of Technology Education* 7, no. 9 (1995).

Hearn, Michael R. "Embedding a Librarian in the Classroom: An Intensive Information Literacy Model." *Reference Services Review* 33, no. 2 (2005): 219–27.

Manus, Sara J. Beutter. (2009). "Librarian in the Classroom: An Embedded Approach to Music Information Literacy for First-Year Undergraduates." *Notes* 66, no. 2 (2009): 249–61.

Marton, Ference, and Shirley A. Booth. *Learning and Awareness*. Hillside, NJ: Laurence Erlbaum, 1997.

McGuinness, Claire. "What Faculty Think—Exploring the Barriers to Information Literacy Development in Undergraduate Education." *The Journal of Academic Librarianship* 32, no. 6 (2006): 573–82.

———. "Exploring Strategies for Integrated Information Literacy: From 'Academic Champions' to Institution-Wide Change." *Communications in Information Literacy* 1, no. 1 (2007): 26–38.

Vincent, Annette, and Dianne Ross. "Learning Style Awareness." *Journal of Research on Computing in Education* 33, no. 5 (2001): 1–10.

Webber, Sheila, and Bill Johnston. "Conceptions of Information Literacy: New Perspectives and Implications." *Journal of Information Science* 26, no. 6 (2000): 381–97.

9
Setting Personal Goals

Our goals can only be reached through a vehicle of a plan,
in which we must fervently believe, and upon which we must
vigorously act. There is no other route to success.

—Pablo Picasso

ONE IS NOT AN EMBEDDED LIBRARIAN AS MUCH AS ONE BE-
comes an embedded librarian. This is a process that is ever evolving and
will change based upon a large number of factors. Faculty, students, subjects,
and settings can all change from semester to semester, so it is good to be flexible, but flexibility does not preclude the planning and setting of goals. This
became painfully evident to me the first time I embedded in a class. Things
went much better in so many ways once I was clearer about what I wanted to
learn, know, and achieve for myself and, as well, what I wanted and expected
in student outcomes. Despite so much of the literature on embedded librarianship (including this book), success is still very much dependent upon the
way in which any particular librarian wishes to envision him or herself in the
classroom experience.

After evaluating myself after a few years, I realized there were certain
aspects of the embedding practice that either required or benefited from formalized personal goals. While so many of us carry expectations of ourselves
around in our heads, it is helpful to write down your goals—indeed, your personal vision for the work that you will do, because most of all, doing so con-
cretizes these goals, making you more likely to do what you need to do to see
them through.

In my own case, I even went as far as to write my own mini-mission statement which kept me focused and inspired me during the times when I felt that things were not going as well as I wanted them to—or as well as I *thought* they should. Guided by the pioneering work of Latham and Locke, who cited the five aspects of goal setting as clarity, challenge, commitment, feedback, and task complexity,[1] have set down some strategies and goals for goal setting (yes, goals for goal setting!) that will help in the formation of your teaching plan.

STRATEGIES AND GOALS

Strategy

Meet with the professor early and often in the process. Team teaching at its best is difficult to get just right. And students can always tell when it isn't working. Team teaching implies just that: teamwork, with both professors coming to the class with the same agenda. In an embedded classroom, things work a bit differently. There will be times when you may feel as though you are just another student in class. You may be reluctant to interject comments or suggestions at critical moments—that is understandable. Discuss this with the professor and state exactly how you envision your participation in class. Will the professor assign time to you at the beginning or end of the class? Will you lead discussions, in-class brainstorming sessions? In other words, is it your goal to be fully "functional" in the class, and if so, how?

> ### GOAL
>
> Open and honest communication with the professor in class is important, with expectations placed front and center.

Strategy

Meet with each student in the class individually. Ideally, this should be arranged during the first two weeks of classes in order to establish a connection. I do five-minute sessions that are non-threatening because I seek an exchange of information. I ask students certain questions, such as what their concerns are for their thesis, what text they may want to use, and how, specifically, I may be able to help them in class. In the beginning, sometimes a student and I would simply brainstorm. They can ask me questions, too, which they often do, one of which is "Why do you need to attend class with us?" This is an interesting yet disappointing question, as it placed me, the librarian, in a passive role—as "one of the crowd." It also alerted me, early on, that while I was very clear in my own head about what my role was, it was largely a mystery to students who only encountered me behind the reference desk or in a 45-minute information literacy session.

GOAL

Recognize and attempt to understand students' goals for the class individually, and communicate how you can help them in their process.

Strategy

Keep a file of notes on each student. This strategy helped me tremendously, especially since I was embedded in two classes each semester. Each time a student met with me, I was able to keep notes on what particular research concerns they had and what progress they made, if in fact they had made progress. I also wrote down the recommendations and mini-assignments I would give them, usually in the form of how to progress with research, and then I held them accountable for it. I never forgot what we'd discussed, because I had everything written down!

GOAL

Understand student learning as a process and identify areas of difficulty and success.

Strategy

What is it exactly that you'd like to accomplish? When your goals are specific and directed, you are able to deviate from them, and refocus if you need to, but if you are not specific at the outset, your actions will feel rudderless. Be as intentional as possible. The librarian in the classroom has any number of challenges. Visualize those challenges and set your goals in contrast to them.

GOAL

Be as specific as possible when deciding what you seek to accomplish in the classroom.

Strategy

When something is not working, don't be afraid to change course. While we are often urged to "stay the course," it is unnecessary and often detrimental to the class to continue in a manner that feels awkward and to which students or the professor are not responding. This could be anything at all. Being able to recalibrate after what might feel like an unsuccessful class is essential.

GOAL

Be flexible with plans. Dispel fixed ideas.

Strategy

Take notes during each and every class. Note not just subject content, but also student and professor reactions, student comprehension, and process. In fact, write down anything at all that is going to help you to gauge what is working and what is not working in class. This strategy may not be all that intuitive to librarians who are used to going into a class with a lesson plan or notes and then doing student assessment (in some cases), but unless they are embedded, they do not have the opportunity to observe "process." Putting your thoughts and impressions into a narrative is crucial to a practice that will be ever evolving. Keeping a process journal has been indispensable to me because I was able to see patterns, warning signs, and successes that, in retrospect, I was not cognizant of when they were happening.

GOAL

Be reflective of your practice.

Strategy

Goals set should have a measure of complexity. Without a challenge there will not be much to motivate you, though conventional wisdom might dictate that setting simple goals would ensure success by being easier to achieve, but the opposite is true. Attempting to perform a task or achieve a goal breeds motivation, which will keep you focused and intent upon succeeding.

GOAL

Set complex goals, but not so complex as not to be achievable. Go beyond your reach.

Strategy

It is easy to lose perspective on your own performance in the class. When you are in the thick of the semester and knee-deep in research strategies and student meetings you may not feel as though you have the time for self-assessment. Those notes you are taking and that journal you are writing in will make so much more sense to you in retrospect. In meetings with the professor in the class, ask for honest feedback by asking specific questions about areas that may be of concern. In my own experience, the professors that I have worked with and I both had similar learning outcome goals for the class—and in nearly every instance, they were willing to help me with my personal goals, as well, because they too would impact the class.

GOAL

Ask for feedback.

Strategy

Embedded librarians are largely committed to the unknown. This means that we are constantly recalibrating and readjusting as we go along in the process. This implies more than just the regular commitment, because we are outside of our regular routines, and while we are tasked to teach in the class and the students are ours, they are not "ours" alone.

GOAL

Commit to the unknown.

FINAL THOUGHTS

Setting goals for what you want to achieve will not only help you to visualize success, but will give you something to strive toward. So much time and energy go into the role of the embedded librarian in the classroom, and the setting of goals helps one to be strategic, intentional, and ultimately, successful.

NOTE

1. Edwin A. Locke and Gary P. Latham, *A Theory of Goal Setting & Task Performance* (Upper Saddle Brook, NJ: Prentice-Hall, 1990).

RESOURCES

Eccles, Jacquelynne S., and Allan Wigfield. "Motivational Beliefs, Values, and Goals." *Annual Review of Psychology* 53, no. 1 (2002): 109–32.

Locke, Edwin A. "Toward a Theory of Task Motivation and Incentives." *Organizational Behavior and Human Performance* 3, no. 2 (1968): 157–89.

Locke, Edwin A. and Gary P. Latham. *A Theory of Goal Setting & Task Performance*. Upper Saddle Brook, NJ: Prentice-Hall College Division, 1990.

10
Personal Branding in Embedded Librarianship

The secret of change is to focus all of your energy, not on fighting the old, but on building the new.

—Socrates

IN VARIOUS PLACES IN THIS BOOK I HAVE REFERRED TO THE difficulty librarians encounter regarding their image. There is a landfill of literature on the topic, and out-of-date and sometimes offensive stereotypes not only persist, but are also still actively applied to our profession. The misunderstood nature of what we do is stubbornly persistent, and I have long tired of trying to tell people what I do to faculty, students, and friends alike. Justification to others takes a lot of energy and, in the end, just does not make a difference. When I made the transition into embedded librarianship, I felt it was a great fit for me, personally, long before I believe it convinced others who simply did not understand. I would turn up the corner of my lips in a strained smile at the questions or the references to embedded journalists. In essence, I have always believed that the best advertisement for what we do is to do it, and engage in it the best way possible every single day. The years leading up to my role as an embedded librarian and the semesters actually spent doing it did not widely change the perception of librarians, particularly on campus, but it helped. I realized that a more strategic approach was in order and I began to explore ways to exploit what I was doing in a personal way that people could connect to and understand, since the concepts would be attached to me personally, and then understood in a wider, more global way. As my director has always said, "What is good for one librarian is good for us all."[1]

Mon and Harris[2] have written about the "invisibility" of the librarian and the difficulties of recognition despite our best efforts. Obviously simply doing what we do is not good enough. My own strategies came out of my frustration of being consistently misunderstood by nearly everyone that I was not working directly with. And I knew that if I could successfully market my own practice, it would help to provide both a framework and a platform for my colleagues, each of whom, though not (yet) fully embedded, continues to embrace many of the principles and practices of embedded librarianship in their respective liaison departments.

Personal branding, far from being a narcissistic pursuit, is an important step in creating your professional self. Rampersad calls one's personal brand "the synthesis of all the expectations, images, and perceptions it creates in the minds of others when they see or hear your name."[3] He goes on to give examples of several people who upon simply hearing a person's name can evoke the essence of their professional lives, such as Tiger Woods, Bill Gates, Einstein, and Mother Teresa. And while it would have been unlikely that Mother Teresa would have even thought of professionally branding herself, the work that she did in the slums of Calcutta and her authenticity did that for her. Rampersad goes on to say, "Your personal brand should be authentic; reflect your true character; and be built on your values, strengths, uniqueness, and genius. If you are branded in this organic, authentic, and holistic way, your personal brand will be strong, clear, complete, and valuable to others." I would add that it could also influence, in the right direction, decision makers and others.[4]

While many librarians may recoil at the term *customers* as it is applied, particularly to those we serve in academia, in essence that is what they are. We can call them patrons, customers, or either, though because I work in a university, I call them "students" and "faculty." I believe that when we are "selling" or "marketing" ourselves, terms matter; in fact, they matter a lot. Calling those we teach "customers" places us, once again, in the mind's eye simply and solely in the position of being limited to provide "service." This is perhaps even more detrimental in the case of embedded librarianship, where we strive to fully collaborate in the teaching/learning cycle and to encourage future collaboration as well. Those providing service (those in true service professions would most likely attest to this) are rarely seen as equals, or in fact, consciously respected, by those whom they serve. If promoting embedded librarianship is to consist of, among other things, personal selling techniques and branding, then the way we see ourselves in our roles and the way we communicate that to those in our campus community is important. It starts with us, with who we are.

PERSONAL SELLING POINTS

One of the most interesting aspects of collaboration with faculty in the classroom is *being* one of the actual faculty in the classroom. At my university my colleagues and I are ranked as assistant professors, and though I think the tide is turning, few see us as true equals, and some might question if we really are. Many discussions among us have been focused on how we are to "be" assistant professors; in other words, how do we enact our roles so that we are seen to be "fit" for our titles? When thinking about marketing, our services, our libraries, and ourselves, actually cast us in a different light. Faculty, for instance, have no need for advertising, per se, unless it is for a new course offering. How do embedded librarians promote themselves and their services in a dignified, attractive, and enticing way? If librarians would engage in personal branding, they will not only promote themselves, but their services as well.

A recurring theme in this book and one of the most important aspects of embedded librarianship is the fact that relationships are of the utmost importance when attempting to both begin and maintain such a deep interconnected collaboration. Ulla de Stricker, information consultant, drives this point home when she asserts: "Let me just say it now: Marketing isn't our issue. Relationships are. Marketing is misunderstood and misplaced if it isn't seen as a natural consequence of everything else we do. . . . In other words, if relationships are done right, marketing takes care of itself."[5]

Finley points to "mixed concepts" in marketing techniques for librarians, but makes a distinction with what he terms *personal selling* since "it provides opportunities to interact directly with the customer."[6] Again, while I object to the term *customer*, I believe that any time a librarian can effectively communicate with those we seek to collaborate with, the better it is. A personal brand is about embracing the totality of who you are as a person and a professional.

In my own practice I used personal selling techniques to not only "advertise" my services and those of the library, but to also increase confidence in the capability of my colleague librarians in general. We have recognized the need to be more high-profile, not only in our professional pursuits on campus, but in campus activities and committees as well. When the campus community knows who you are in another context, they are more likely to reach out to you for your services as a colleague.

One of my colleagues, Calvin, is an extremely social person, perhaps the most social among us. The rest of us, in our own way, could be seen as the prototypical or stereotypical librarians—a bit on the quiet side, spectacled and focused. But Calvin, from the beginning, was a different breed. As our university's only science librarian he has his work cut out for him, as he liaises, by himself, with the most departments both on campus and our campuses off-site. He has been encouraging all of us for years to integrate ourselves into the campus more fully. He serves on various committees, does an incredible amount of information literacy sessions, and likes to hobnob with just about anyone. On any given day he would be playing Frisbee on the Haber Green, the beautiful lawn area that is the center of campus, with any number of students, or riding his unicycle and waving to just about everyone that he sees. Calvin has softened and humanized the perception of himself as a librarian and has been able to make many inroads into various collaborative efforts on campus. Others and I believe that he has been so successful in his efforts because he puts himself forward in ways that are open and welcoming. He believes that being so well integrated personally on campus has helped him to be successful professionally. In fact, I credit Calvin with helping to move us in the direction of the high-profile status on campus that we enjoy today. While Calvin has never spoken in particular of "branding" in regard to his personal and professional self, it is clear to those who know him (which is just about everyone) that he is an authentic person, professionally invested in his work. All of the aspects of Calvin's personality and activities reflect the act of branding.

In my own experience my route to embedded librarianship was not at all straightforward. I was known on campus, but not half as integrated as I would have liked to be, as I knew I *needed* to be. And I was very sure that I did not want my embedding experience to be a one-off, and that I wanted to be able to develop a professional and academic collaborative practice that would be sustainable. And that meant that I needed buy-in from those I wanted to work with and the department in which they resided. Since we were not ready to institute an actual embedded *program* on campus, personal selling techniques and personal branding made more sense to me than traditional "marketing" strategies. People needed to know me, and I had to distinguish myself, though not in a phony, trumped-up way, but instead, I needed to express myself by integrating my personal and professional personas. I aimed to build trust with the campus community in an intentional and thoughtful way. Branding is not a series of homemade posters, fliers tacked up in the dining hall or on classroom walls, games or gimmicks more suited to elementary classrooms, or any other number of outdated ways that librarians used to tout themselves and library services. I remember one librarian telling me with pride that at her small university library, everyone who checked out a laptop got a lollipop—she called it "Lollipops and Laptops"—so as to build a friendly reputation with students. While well meaning, this does nothing to dispel the persistent stereotypes and can actually do more harm personally and to the profession in the long run. And while being friendly and approachable is an admirable goal for anyone in any profession, and we definitely aim for that, doing so in a way that respects our users' experience is of the utmost importance.

STRATEGIES FOR BRANDING

Know who you are: Does this seem obvious? It should be, but in a world full of image-making, artifice, and the cult of the personality, people are often more conscious of who they *want* to be, and often not in a thoughtful and constructive way—but instead, they want to be who they are not; and that, we know, never works. *Know* who you are and *be* who you are. Write down your good qualities and exploit them. Write down your weak points and vow to work on them. Authenticity is an incredibly attractive quality in a person. And when you are who you say you are, you will exude trust and show yourself trustworthy. And relationships are built and maintained on trust.

Love what you do: If you don't, you are in the wrong profession. Anything less than love and it will show on your face and in the work that you do.

Dedicate yourself to what you do: It takes time and dedication to do our jobs well. I remember being told in high school by a teacher I greatly admired that those with jobs tend to be unhappy because they do them out of necessity, not out of love. A profession is something you train for, are educated to become. Librarians have been educated to do what we do. Professional development, conferences, and collaboration with colleagues, among other strategies, will enhance your professional life and those with whom you come in contact in your campus community.

Identify who you want to reach: Branding is meant to communicate an integrated self, but there will be a department on campus that you may want to target in order to develop a working relationship. Craft the way you communicate your target group, which may have different objectives than another group. You will still be who you are, but your communication will be shaped in a different way for your target group.

Be clear about what you would like to communicate and cultivate your communication style: I can be chatty with those I know, but I'd rather listen.

Create short-term and long-term strategies for developing your brand: I am a dyed-in-the-wool introvert and shy, but I happen to be very gregarious in the library. Out of it, not so much. I decided as a short-term goal that it would be easier to get to know faculty by engaging them in a friendly atmosphere, where we could get to know one another. I decided that showing up in the faculty dining room would place me in situations that were not intimidating to me. This short-term goal worked and help to ease me into the long-term goal of working more closely with my liaison departments.

Be consistent: Be who you are every day. Inconsistency in any way will tarnish your professional reputation and create confusion as to who you are and what you represent.

Recognize that your brand is your reputation and nothing less: Your reputation is everything. And once it is damaged, it is a long climb back to respectability and trust.

FINAL THOUGHTS

The cover of a recent *The Nation* issue featured an article on librarians challenging the National Security Agency and had a title that proclaimed: "Not your grandmother's librarian!" The profession has gone through a sea change in recent years, and it is time that our brands caught up with those changes. One can see evidence of branding nearly everywhere. Branding has been around for a long time and can be misunderstood as egoism, which it is not. Branding is the controlling and managing of the information we want others to know about us. For embedded librarians in the classroom, that is an invaluable aspect of what we do: when we do what we do in the best way that we can, students and faculty alike will notice. And talk about it!

NOTES

1. Personal conversation with Dr. Jeanne Buckley, Arcadia University.
2. Lorri Mon and Lydia Eato Harris, "The Death of the Anonymous Librarian," *The Reference Librarian* 52, no. 4 (2011): 352–64.
3. Hubert K. Rampersad, "A New Blueprint for Powerful and Authentic Personal Branding," *Performance Improvement* 47, no. 6 (2008): 34–37.
4. Ibid.
5. Ulla de Stricker, "Relationships R Us: Climbing Up the Value Chain," *Information Outlook* 4, no. 11 (2000): 30–33.
6. Wayne E. Finley, "Using Personal Selling Techniques in Embedded Librarianship," *Journal of Business & Finance Librarianship* 18, no. 4 (2013): 281.

RESOURCES

Badke, William. "Why Information Literacy Is Invisible." *Communications in Information Literacy* 4, no. 2 (2011): 129–41.

De Saez, Eileen Elliott. *Marketing Concepts for Libraries and Information Services*. 2nd ed. London: Facet, 2002.

Finley, Wayne E. "Using Personal Selling Techniques in Embedded Librarianship." *Journal of Business & Finance Librarianship* 18, no. 4 (2013): 279–92.

Gall, Dan. "Librarian like a Rock Star: Using Your Personal Brand to Promote Your Services and Reach Distant Users." *Journal of Library Administration* 52, nos. 6-7 (2012): 549–58.

Knight, Valerie R., and Charrisa Loftis. "Moving from Introverted to Extraverted Embedded Librarian Services: An Example of a Proactive Model." *Journal of Library & Information Services in Distance Learning*, 6, nos. 3-4 (2012): 362–75.

Kranich, Nancy, Megan Lotts, and Gene Springs. "The Promise of Academic Libraries Turning Outward to Transform Campus Communities." *College & Research Libraries News* 75, no. 4 (2014): 182–86.

Markgren, Susanne. "Ten Simple Steps to Create and Manage Your Professional Online Identity: How to Use Portfolios and Profiles." *College & Research Libraries News* 72, no. 1 (2011): 31–35.

Mon, Lorri, and Lydia Eato Harris. "The Death of the Anonymous Librarian." *The Reference Librarian* 52, no. 4 (2011): 352–64.

Nalani Meulemans, Yvonne, and Allison Carr. "Not at Your Service: Building Genuine Faculty-Librarian Partnerships." *Reference Services Review* 41, no. 1 (2013): 80–90.

Pell, John, Sarah Ward, and Margaret Bausman. "Can't Get No Satisfaction: Lessons Learned While Developing an Assessment of Faculty Awareness and Attitudes toward Library Services." In conference proceedings of the City University of New York Office of Library Services Conference, *Reinventing Libraries: Reinventing Assessment: Innovative Practices and Ideas That Challenge the Status Quo, June*, vol. 19 (2014).

Shea, Erin. "Taking Stock of Your Institution's Marketing Efforts." *Reference & User Services Quarterly* 54, no. 3 (2015): 27.

11
Being Embedded

An Odyssey

*One does not discover new lands without consenting
to lose sight of the shore for a very long time.*

—André Gide

EMBEDDED LIBRARIANSHIP NECESSITATES THE STEPPING OUT of an old, comfortable role and embarking on a new way of being, without the safety net of known results. When I made the decision to embed, there was so much that I did not know, so many guarantees that I could not make to myself, students, or the professors I worked with. I needed to rely on the growing feeling that there was a better way, that I could initiate something on my own that, while needing the permission of my library director and the support of my colleagues, I needed no particular mandate to get started.

I had been playing in the arena of embedded librarianship for quite some time—in actuality, about five years before I was actually able to embed fully. Working with different professors in different classes was akin to putting a lot of small and jagged pieces together in order to be able to see an emerging pattern. I met with so many different obstacles, objections, misunderstandings, and false starts. It made me realize, with more clarity than ever before, how librarians are thought of in the academic environment if, in fact, they are even thought of at all.

I actually had what I would call a "mixed bag" of obstacles. Since I am the English department liaison, it seemed, on the face of it, natural that I would embed in the Senior Thesis course and the required course for the major,

"Interpreting Literature." The library director was supportive and trusted me to come up with a workable plan. I had dabbled in "decentralizing" service by setting up regular reference hours in the Commons, a new building on campus that was a center of various aspects of student activity, including a food court. I would have a table, my laptop, and a bowl of candy. Word of mouth would spread this service, and because I enjoyed a friendly and cordial relationship with so many students on campus, I assumed this endeavor could be nothing but wildly successful. My colleagues were not all that interested in sharing shifts with me, but supported me, nonetheless. I would show up, feeling kind of puffed up with what I assumed was a great idea (I'd been reading about it in library literature for quite some time) and got a lot of reactions—none of them particularly helpful or appreciated. Students seemed rather confused about why I was there. Mostly, the students would come to the table for hard candy or chocolate that I provided as a thinly disguised lure. I actually managed to turn some casual and friendly conversations into research encounters, but they were very clearly contrived on my part (as anyone could see), and, admittedly, they were few and far between. Of course I believed in reaching out to students, and was intrigued by "meeting students where they are" (even if I did know *where* they were) and desperate for the chance, even if I had to find my own way to do it. When I was asked to provide statistics for the service, which were dismal, I decided, with very strong suggestion from the director, to abandon the ill-conceived idea. Nobody missed it.

Eventually, it became an exercise in futility to simply hang the proverbial shingle out advertising my services in an atmosphere where students clearly wanted to do a lot of things (eat, play pool, socialize, study, etc.), but actual research with a librarian was not one of them. And that is okay. I actually had begun to feel as though I was invading their space. I reasoned to myself that I had tried the idea and it didn't work. At the time I felt some acute disappointment and some embarrassment since I'd been so vocal about decentralizing service to all who would listen. But, looking back now, I see that I was thinking in the right direction. That what I desired was an out-of-the-box way of reaching students. No more dabbling. Thus began what I have always thought of as the odyssey toward being embedded in the classroom. And after my experiences, I can claim not only to *think* of embedding as an odyssey, through my experiences, but I can claim it as one!

A BUMPY START

After my failure at taking reference services out of the library, I recalibrated. It was the end of the spring semester, and I decided that the time was right to approach the professor who would be teaching the English Thesis course in the fall. This professor, just two years away from retirement, was a noted scholar.

He was also recognized as probably the most traditional in the English department. In fact, he'd been my undergraduate thesis professor many years before! In many ways, I thought that the fact that I was the department's liaison and had, myself, graduated from the very program that I was seeking to embed in, would make things very easy for me: that I would be welcomed unreservedly and fully trusted. Nothing could have been further from the truth. While I would not venture to say in this case that familiarity bred contempt, exactly, it certainly did not open the doors that I thought it would.

I sat on the edge of the old wooden chair, facing the professor. It was five o'clock in the afternoon and the sun coming through his cloudy office windows blended uneasily with the fluorescent lighting. He rummaged through a voluminous amount of papers piled haphazardly and, without looking at me, said in his very precise and clipped voice, "Well, go ahead, Michelle. I am listening." I was not encouraged, but I forged ahead, nonetheless.

"I'd like to be embedded in your Thesis course in the fall." The papers continued to shuffle, he dropped his pen on the floor, and the department secretary poked her head into his office to say "goodnight" for the day. He looked up and smiled at her and returned the "goodnight." He looked at me as though seeing me for the first time.

When I began to unfold my rationale and then my plan, I am not sure what I expected, but I know it was not the reaction I received.

"Michelle [he pronounced my name "Mee-shell"], thesis students are seniors. They know how to do research." This was clearly going to be one of the major sticking points: convincing him that it simply was not true. That in fact, I usually found seniors no better at research than they were in their sophomore year—just one of the reasons I felt that I needed to become closer, both literally and figuratively, to the students' experience, perspective, and practice.

I attempted to lay out a rationale and then a plan for the fall semester, but became rather tongue-tied and anxious, which he seemed to notice. With a heavy sigh, he told me it was a lot to think about. He would be off to London for research in a few days and he promised me he'd check back in with me upon his return. In fact, defying my expectations, he did contact me. He reluctantly agreed to allow me to "embed"—"whatever that is," he mused. While on the face of it, it *seemed* like a victory of sorts, it didn't feel like one. At that moment, I did not have any idea of how challenging being embedded in a classroom with a professor who, despite my efforts, still had no clear idea of what I wanted to achieve with my idea and whose confidence in the process and the entire enterprise was dubious at best. I spent the summer thinking about and planning my course of action. I attempted to communicate with the professor twice toward the end of the summer, though I received no reply until the second day of the fall semester. I asked that my professional information and contact e-mail and phone extension be placed on the syllabus.

I crafted a short paragraph that sought to explain to students why I was in the class and how I aimed to help them with their research. I explained that I felt "contextualizing" my presence would help to ensure the success of my mission. He denied both requests, reasoning that the students knew how to contact me if, in fact, they needed me and furthermore, I should just *do* what I needed to do instead of talking about it. Not an auspicious start, but I forged ahead. He *had* consented to let me be there, after all. I seriously thought that the biggest hurdle had been overcome.

THE BEGINNING OF A LONG ROAD

I sat among the nineteen students in the long seminar room. Each student was instructed to introduce themselves and tell the class which text they'd chosen for their thesis. When it came to be my turn, the professor introduced me and told the class that I would occasionally be in class to help them with their research. I scanned the faces in the room and saw mild boredom and amusement. My presence, at that point, seemed not to make a bit of difference, except maybe to pique some curiosity. While the concept of the "embedded" librarian was not explained to them, as I had been hoping to do, they had never experienced a librarian in a classroom. For the next few weeks, to say that my efforts were marginalized is to put it mildly. Each class would begin in the same way: with the professor exclaiming great surprise that I would be joining them that day. It became a running joke. I wonder if those of you reading this right now might judge me by my seeming passivity in the classroom, most especially because it seems as though I was consistently being disrespected in very insidious ways, though to be fair to the professor, now retired, I don't think he meant it as severely as it came off. I knew that to climb this mountain, which is how I had begun to think of the Thesis class, I needed to stick it out. I knew that it would be far from easy, so I was willing to sacrifice my ego in the service of long-term goals. So I began a sort of ethnographic approach and began taking meticulous notes on student behavior and in-class questions, expressed areas of difficulty, and classroom discussions as they unfolded in class. Thankfully, I was meeting with the students one-on-one in my office regularly, so I was able to collect a lot of information directly from them, and help them work through their Achilles heels.

It took an almost Herculean effort not to insert myself more forcefully in the class. There were so many practices that I thought might be effective, but doing so would have severely thrown the class off balance and would have seemed disjointed (and possibly contentious) in a way that most students would have been able to pick up on. A talk with the director galvanized my direction: it was all about them and not about me. I resolved to do what I could with the limited time and access to the students that were allotted to me.

After a semester of being in the class, I can say that I reached about 90 percent of the class and by that, I mean that is the percentage that took the initiative to come to me for help, even though it was an *unwritten* rule that each student would meet with me *at least* twice during the semester; the professor had not wanted to have to commit to anything on paper.

While the professor was not all that enthusiastic to "debrief" me at the end of the semester, he did casually mention to me in the spring, after the thesis projects were graded, that he felt that the final projects showed a "marked improvement" from the last few years, certainly the previous year, and while he did not attribute that directly to me, I was pleased nonetheless. More importantly, it was just enough feedback to put me back in the saddle again for the following semester, with a new professor, while the previous one was on sabbatical. I resolved to be flexible, though more intentional in my practice.

SELF-ASSESSMENT

I felt as though the semester had drained me. While I enjoyed a wonderful working relationship with the English department, I was worried that my experience in the Thesis class would have been looked upon negatively by the professor that I worked with, a man who was greatly (and deservedly) respected, but a bit "old school." In order to gain perspective on what I had been trying to achieve, I decided that I knew very well what didn't work—and my own predominant feeling was that I simply was not given permission to do what I could have done in the class. Period. I decided to turn that corner quickly and focus on what did work. And there were more than a few things in this area.

What I could not implement in class, I did in one-on-one consultations. I understood early on that all I would be able to do in class, for the most part, would be to observe, but I made it work. Because my notes were so pithy, I had a keen insight into where students seemed to be having difficulties and where they seemed to do just fine. When students came to my office, *we worked*. And I recognized and respected different learning styles. From brainstorming ideas, annotated bibliographies, developing keywords for database searching, and everything else in between, information literacy was at the forefront.

I was a constant source of support. The students realized that soon enough. Because the class was largely a class based in literary theory, much of the class content was delivered through lecture, with a bit of discussion. Because I was receiving the same information that the students were, I understood where they were and where they should be. When they would meet with me in person, they would often refer to something in class that I had an immediate reference point for. There was no guessing on my part, not the usual request for me to see the assignment. I was there. One student said that coming to me for help was such a relief, in part because she didn't have to "fill in all the blanks" for me—I could usually understand when a student was having difficulties. I vowed to be responsive to e-mails on the weekend, which is when many of the students actually did their homework and worked on drafts of their papers. I would often check in with students to see how their drafts were coming, or to follow up on our sessions, sometimes just to give encouragement. The majority of the class reached out—and often.

I never missed a class. Embedded librarianship is time-consuming, of that there is no doubt. It is a major commitment. I must admit that during the first few weeks I felt more than a bit superfluous, but I resisted the urge to pack it all in. I was committed to it and remembered my director's mantra: "It's not about you." And so, while in nearly every class one or more students would be absent, I never was, an aspect that I am quite proud of. If I could stick through a situation that was not ideal (but had potential), then I was going to do that. I never regretted it and feel as though the time was well spent. While not every embedded librarian will feel the need to attend every class session, it helped me to begin to construct a way of being a librarian in a classroom; with each and every class session I gained so much insight into the students and how they learn and how I could impact that learning.

I built relationships with students that impacted their learning. A theme that I return to again and again in this book is that of relationship building in embedded librarianship. The old adage "relationships are everything" can be perfectly applied in this context. When the group dynamics finally began to unfold in the class and we all became more or less comfortable as a group, I felt that students did not need to pretend that they understood things that they didn't. I have often thought that we have made too much of the "digital native"—and that we have endowed students with a false sense of their technological superiority. I have seen this enacted over the reference desk when a student will come to ask for my help, but become defensive when I ask what strategies, for instance, they have already employed, which must sound to them as though I am implying that they do not know what they are doing. In fact, sometimes they don't. I suppose if they did, they would not ask for help. The difference in the embedded class was that they got to know me, and I got to know them, so we had a base of understanding from which to work. I have had students cry in my office out of sheer frustration and mental exhaustion, students that had such "senioritis" that they did not even think they had the wherewithal to complete a thesis. We have all been there. Librarians know the student meltdown as well as anyone—probably even better than their own professors do, since we almost always see them in a moment of crisis or desperation—and sadly, often as the last resort. Because students came to know me in the same way they would come to know anyone that they were taking a class with, they felt comfortable coming to me for help. The quality of their final projects that the professor claimed to see, compared to years past, could be said to be a result of this.

I demystified the role of a librarian. This is important. Fear of librarians is real and so is library anxiety. I am human, so I acted like it. I provided a sounding board for students to verbalize their thought processes and figure out the next step in research before I stepped in. I wanted to empower them and I could not do that by dazzling them with my bag of research tricks. More than a few students knew that I, too, was a researcher and would ask me about my process. I was not afraid to tell them that often my process looked a lot like theirs: all over the place. That yes, indeed, I used Google and, in fact, when I need to understand a complicated concept or familiarize myself with a topic I knew nothing about, I would consult (gasp!) Wikipedia. I emphasized that librarians did not *have* all the answers, but we were very good at knowing where to *find* them. I aligned myself with them in their research struggle and allowed them the luxury of finding their way—which meant that they would make mistakes, they would struggle and become frustrated. It also meant that they would see that research is never as easy as they'd like it to be. I aimed to show by example.

I strengthened my relationship with my liaison department. I proved that I had both the content knowledge (holding both undergraduate and graduate degrees in English, though this is not a prerequisite) and the competence to lead students toward a satisfying and productive research/learning experience. While respected, I did not always feel (and this feeling was shared by my colleagues) that faculty truly understood what it is, exactly, that we are capable of doing. While the professor in my class may have felt threatened, in some way, by my presence or he may have felt that my contributions could not have made much of a difference, in the end he spoke enthusiastically to those in his department about my efforts. Word-of-mouth testimonials are perhaps the best, and I felt encouraged by the fact that in the end my efforts were constructive and appreciated.

This was the foundation I had hoped for and would prove fruitful in helping me to make further headway into the department.

I was invited to a department meeting to speak about my experience with the thesis class. This turned out to be my chance not only to talk with the English faculty about what I did in the class, but also what was possible in future classes. Because faculty often assume that librarians simply teach "skills," I disabused them of that notion and encouraged them to talk to students who had been in the class, which the chair of the department did. While I could not yet see myself embedded in the actual department, I very much desired to be permanently embedded in the Thesis class and spoke in detail about strategies for the class. I expressed a sincere desire to be an educational partner with the end goal of student success.

Students thanked me with sincerity. I mourned the end of the class, even though I found it exhausting. The ramp-up to beginning a new practice is intense to be sure, but eventually the students and I worked our way into the ebb and flow of the class and when it was over, I felt a bit of relief, but also a void. However, much to my surprise I was rewarded with e-mails thanking me for my help, as well as students who would drop by the library just to say "hello." This was incredibly gratifying to me, and more than their good grades, made me realize that I'd made a difference in some way.

The success of my first semester as an embedded (though not fully integrated) librarian was one of learning how to function within limits and aspiring to greater growth within the mandate that I had set for myself. As I will show, often the success of any endeavor, particularly being embedded in a class, comes in increments. It is hard to gauge the success of efforts during a semester, when one's nose is to the grindstone. Enlightenment about your own process and your own assessment of your performance will come in increments, too. It helps to share the experience with your colleagues, just as we encourage our students to talk to each other about research, because feedback is an important part of any practice. My colleagues were incredibly helpful in listening patiently to my triumphs as well as my moments when I felt that the entire enterprise was doomed from the outset. I was (and still am) my university's only embedded librarian, and while my colleagues don't yet have an interest in embedding as fully as I have and in the way that I have, they have been incredibly supportive of my efforts. When in the throes of an odyssey, that support means just about everything and I am grateful for it.

AN EMBEDDED LIBRARIAN GROWS SEA LEGS

The following fall, I was embedded, once again, in the English Thesis seminar, but this time it was taught by another professor with whom I had always enjoyed a good working relationship. We met a few times at odd intervals in the summer where he expressed his being "totally on board" with my being embedded in his class. Interestingly, he laughed lightly one day and said, "I hope you won't be bored!" This took me aback a bit, but the fact that even faculty we have worked closely with continue to misunderstand our mission should not surprise most librarians reading this. I told him that I would be far too busy to be bored at all. I was able to make it clearer to him than I had in my previous experience that I had both goals for my students and myself. And I laid them all out. For me to be able to achieve in the classroom what I'd planned, I would need a (small) portion of class time—regularly.

Because I felt more confident this time around, I was more assertive in my approach right from the beginning, an approach that the professor appreciated. I told him that I would introduce myself during the first class and lay out my expectations, both of what they could expect from me and I from them. I knew many of the students in the class, as I'd encountered them in other English classes in which I did sessions, so I found the atmosphere immediately comfortable and welcoming.

The atmosphere in the class was a relaxed one due to the fact that the professor combined lectures with a large amount of class discussion, creating a balance that resonated with the students.

Because I felt deprived of the proper contextualization the first time around, I stood in front of the class this time and laid out my plan. My name and contact information were included on the syllabus, and I was ready to dig into the semester.

The English Thesis class (EN490) is, for students, a rather uncomfortable blend of theory and thesis writing. Beyond the EN299 class in which theory and synthesizing research is prominent, they are encouraged but not required to use theoretical approaches in other English classes. By the time students get to their senior year, two things come as a shock: the actual writing of a thesis along with having to both (re)learn theory and apply it to their paper. This presents a few challenges. Students have felt that the actual writing of the thesis is sacrificed at the altar of theory. Discussion and assignments, including reaction papers to the large amount of readings that they do, they feel, detract from the writing of their thesis. And while every attempt is made to have the two topics blend and overlap, there are distinctions that keep them separate.

I understood this on a deep level, since the thesis class has remained virtually unchanged since I received my BA in English at the university. I remember, acutely, feeling so confused at that time—knowing my grade would depend almost entirely on my final project, but receiving no real direction in the process of writing it. Forget the fact that I was an English major and had already written more papers than I can remember. The thesis was different.

In the case of my students, nearly from the beginning of the prior semester, they expressed real concern over the guidance they felt they needed, which I addressed in the ways previously described.

The professor who I was working with was relieved that I would be, along with him, guiding them through the process. I could employ a many-pronged approach to work toward maximum success.

As a librarian, I felt the need to reinforce the fact that I would take them through the project step by step. I passed around what was a very simple "intake" form, where I asked students to name the text they would be using, how they begin research, and so on. One outburst in class jolted me out of my good feelings about what I was about to embark on. A female student, slightly older than traditional age, thrust the form back at me and told the professor she refused to fill it out. A few others expressed concerns. I was stymied. I couldn't begin to fathom what the objection was. I told everyone if they did not want to fill it out that was fine. I explained it wasn't a contract, and they were not held to the text they thought they were going to work on at this moment, but just that it gave me a baseline of information that I felt would help *me* to help *them*. I relate this anecdote here to give readers a bit of a sense of the particular kind of resistance a librarian may encounter—and it does not always come by way of faculty in the classroom. This was not only an issue of anxiety that students felt, but testified, in my opinion, to the kind of authority they perceived me to lack in the class. One could not imagine they would challenge the professor in the same way, and of course, they didn't. This was a battle not worth fighting. I would have them come around in other ways.

GETTING DOWN TO WORK

I felt strongly that so much of the anxiety the students felt right at the beginning was because they could not let go of the fact that in fourteen weeks, they would need to produce a draft of a thesis and then would only have about eight weeks into the spring semester for revision, but would not have the benefit of in-class support, though of course I would be there if they needed me. I needed to pry their focus from simply the end result, which they were fixated upon. It seemed huge to them. I needed to build a bridge for them between the process and the product. Time and time again, I have seen students believe that a paper is simply a matter of amassing information that they will haphazardly sift through to prove an already predetermined conclusion. Research is done to know, to find out. We begin writing to know that we are on the right track—or we aren't, and if we aren't going in the right direction we continue to research and think and process.

I was lucky to be working with a professor who was a wonderful proponent of process. He believed in it and he reinforced the *idea* of it. I was there to make that process actually happen. At the professor's preference, we did not use any learning management system in the class, so all interaction took place in person—in the classroom, computer lab, or in my office. Later in the semester, when students were deep into the actual writing of the thesis, I answered a lot of e-mail questions, which were really thinly veiled appeals for moral support. I was happy to oblige!

Roughly the first half of the semester was reimmersing the students in literary theory. This involved a lot of reading and the unraveling of difficult concepts. Usually each week the professor would present a new theory and each student was required to choose one to both present to the class and produce a short paper on. Discussion on theory tended to be intense, with students constantly referring back to their thick theory text and engaging in the conversation. While I took part in the conversations, this was not the part of class that I was most involved with—and yet I still count it as a valuable experience to have been there, because gradually, as I began to lead more sessions directly tied to the writing of the paper, theory would figure prominently.

My sessions with the students in this class were not relegated to the last half-hour, when their minds were tired and they felt rather drained. In fact, this semester had a more organic flow to it, which seemed to work. When we would arrive in class, the professor and I would go over again what each of us aimed to cover and then decide in what order we would do so. I loved when I was able to teach at the start of class. I would begin by taking the class's "temperature"—gauging their mood, and so on, and to see "where they were" mentally and emotionally at that point in their week. This cleared the air a bit.

Nearly all of the students had come into the first class knowing exactly which text they wanted to focus on for their final project, and I liked to give them every opportunity to talk about it. We would go around the room and everyone would state their text and the issue they were going to focus on. I aimed to familiarize students with each other's work, which provoked interest in other topics and approaches. Conversation that leads to in-depth discussion and critical thinking was a crucial component of my time with the class. More often than not, the professor would participate as well, which was fine by me, but I really enjoyed the time when I had them by myself; they were relaxed and more freely expressed their frustrations and difficulties that I needed to be aware of in order to help them. This was also a time when they could, with pride, hold forth on what they did know about their topic, author, or text. These aspects of their work were just as important to share because it served to build their confidence, and afforded them time to connect with one another, not just as peers in the class, but through the challenging process, which they needed, since there was so much that they felt they *didn't* know. As one of the students said, in a dry tone with a straight face, "The struggle is real." It was, but we were all in it together.

ANNOTATED BIBLIOGRAPHIES

As the fall semester got underway, we were all connected to one another, and students were cognizant of one another's project topics. While I have not had much opportunity to give assignments in other classes, I did in this one. I would give the assignments and grade them as well. I have never met a student who enjoyed doing an annotated bibliography, but that was the first assignment, but with a twist. Most librarians are aware of the fact that most students will simply choose the first required number of sources for a bibliography whether or not they are good sources to be able to use *specifically* in their paper. I decided that there would be three stages to this assignment so that students would not be settling for whichever sources they found (because there would be no pressure to do so), but instead would be free to "play the field."

The first annotated bibliography would occur on their "reconnaissance mission." My appeal to them to "just go out there and get the lay of the land" was thought, by the majority of them, to be "busywork." They did not see the point. All I was asking was for them to do some searching in the ballpark of their topic/issue to see what was out there. The purpose of this was to avoid so much of the pointless searching that many students do at this point (searching that is hit or miss) without real evaluation and aiming to use, because they think *anything* rather than *nothing* is useful. I emphasized that they were simply beginning the process and that they should spread the wealth among sources, using a variety such as print and databases. As expected, their sources were very much all over the place, and predominantly digital, which I knew would change as they got further into their research. They were instructed to place their text, topic, and issue at the beginning of their bibliography. I assured them that not only might their issues change as they proceeded further into the research process, but that they *should* change. This was not the backward momentum they perceived it to be, but rather the natural progression of the process. As a freestanding assignment, the sources they listed would have been underwhelming, but I did not consider them so for the first of three bibliographies.

The professor and I were pleased with the first stage of delving into sources. After I had graded and evaluated the assignments, I handed them back and partnered the students up to talk to one another about the assignment. A few students began to panic when they were not satisfied with what they found and thought they might have to change their text, particularly if it was a newer novel they wanted to focus on and there was a lack of critical writing to be found on it. The professor did not have a problem with them changing their texts or topics if they felt strongly about it, but I pointed out to him that they might be doing it for the wrong reasons. Again, the urge to stockpile journal articles like an arsenal during war is a strong one. And while the students needed a certain number of sources for their thesis, their focus needed to be on the *right* sources. I know that students can lose weeks' worth of valuable time when they change their text. They need to start the process over entirely, while others have worked through those issues and are entering into a deeper phase of research.

While week after week theory was at the forefront of the class, I worked with the students to keep the research/writing phase of the class moving forward. They were beginning to develop a conceptual structure to their papers, and I saw them leaning in, becoming truly interested in what they could accomplish. At this time, I started scheduling a fair amount of one-on-one appointments in my office, where the student and I would pick up where we left off in class. And many times, one of two things would happen: I would be able to assure a student that he or she was heading in the right direction (keep doing what you are doing!), or we grappled and worked things out, sometimes taking a direction realized through conversation and talking it out. This is an amazing process, because I gently ask leading questions, and after the first few I don't knows, they are working things out, out loud. They will often answer their own questions. I leave space for their own questioning, their own inquiry. Robert Kegan has noted that learning institutions do a good job of challenging students, but don't do as well in supporting them. He states, "people grow best where they continuously experience an ingenious blend of challenge and support."[1] And so we grappled, we communicated, we shared experiences, we sometimes took three steps forward and two steps back, but this was the research process in all of its glory. I wanted students to be cognizant of the process while they were going through it.

ENTER THEORY INTO WRITING

Because a predominant worry in the class was how divorced the theory portion seemed to be from the actual end game—the actual written thesis, I decided that part of what I would discuss in one of my sessions with the class, about midway through the semester, was how to actually use theory—that is, how to write with a "critical lens." The need to address this concern as part of the process was important because I felt that it was holding them back. As they began what I call the most pleasurable part of the process—finding academic articles on a topic and reading through them—they would express concern that they thought they could write the paper, but they still could not figure out how to make theory fit.

The critical lens exercise would help them to apply that theory. Since they had all read their texts and were quite familiar with them, I told them to choose a chapter or two to tightly focus on. They would locate and highlight specific passages that would seem to support a particular lens. I tried to give simple examples. For instance, one student in the class was working on Margaret Atwood's *A Handmaid's Tale*. I asked the student, to, as explicitly as possible, give us the premise of the book. As she was talking, I could see it dawn on her. "So, I could, like, use a feminist lens, right?" I nodded. "Right," I said. In essence, I told the class, this student would aim to look for particular passages in her chosen chapters that might specifically deal with, for example, the subjugation of a woman's rights, or instances in which a woman was able to triumph over deliberate obstacles placed in her way. I know this sounds as though I was simplifying things, but the students needed a clear and unambiguous example at the outset, because I knew (and they knew) things would get more complicated as they moved along in the process.

Moving along, they would then craft a thesis statement, creating a specific argument about an aspect of the critical lens they would be using and supported by direct quotes from their text. They were told to write an introductory paragraph, which should flow directly from the thesis statement. This paragraph would include concepts that they felt they would need to go into detail that would "set up" the reader for what would follow. An extended version of this assignment would be to then have the students write the body of the essay in paragraphs that would take them deep into the text, analyzing their text from the viewpoint of the critical lens, but in essence, that is exactly what they would be doing when writing their thesis. This exercise served to demystify the act of writing from and through a critical lens.

As with all of the exercises and strategies in class, none of them were done in isolation. Each and every exercise became a talking point, so that everyone was discussing their approach. What I had hoped would happen (and did) was that they began helping each other. For this exercise, no in-depth research was needed, though they did need to familiarize themselves with the theories that they would be working with. Most of the students used the required theory text in the class. This might normally be an exercise that the professor in the class would do with the students, but both he and I reasoned that for me to guide the students in this would flow nicely into all other aspects of the research/writing process of the thesis. And it would be good to point out that while I was the one guiding the exercise, the professor in the class participated in the discussions.

I felt more confident in my role in this class and felt that my relationships with students were progressing in constructive ways. While things were still not as formalized as I would have liked them to be, part of the reason why I describe this practice as an odyssey is that each class will be different, not only perhaps in content or the faculty member that you will be working with, but the students will be different, and the way they react to you in the class and how receptive they are to what you will do in the class will be met with a variety of responses. So while my desire for firmer planning was something that seemed like a good idea in theory, in practice I found that I taught very much what the students needed me to teach. In other words, I responded to their needs as researchers/inquirers instead of trying to make them fit into my preconceived approaches. I offered guidelines and strategies, though a few charted their own course, which was fine.

Then, with some idea of what their theoretical lens would be, we set upon more focused research. I took them to the computer lab twice during the semester. The first time was about six weeks into class where, as I have described earlier in this book, I led the class workshop style. The professor and I would walk around the class helping students with keywords and conceptualizing ideas. I would do a few searches in class, from the podium, but otherwise it was all hands-on. I encouraged them to find at least one article during the lab time, because in my experience, when a student had something in hand, they tended to feel more positive about the search experience and would have a real sense of making progress. Again, I stressed the importance of having the right research, not necessarily a large quantity. While they were senior English majors, I reinforced all of the aspects of evaluating, reading, and synthesizing the information they were gathering, even though they balked a bit. It was not wasted time. The phenomenon of students wanting to find academic articles that spoke to their topic/issue explicitly continued and caused a lot of (in my opinion) unnecessary frustration. But I understood that it was part of the learning process and did the best that I could.

The second annotated bibliography assignment served to concretize their sources so that they were now more specific to their research. And I went a step further in this assignment. While they still had to find and evaluate sources, they had to explain, in very specific terms, why those sources would work for their paper. This would prevent the practice of simply finding any source just to list it and complete the assignment. Many of the students were successful and I was encouraged by the variety of sources as well as their relevance. The students were also mining their sources for other sources, a practice I always encourage. The students had begun to feel as though things were coming into focus, and in fact the professor and I could see evidence of it. They spoke more confidently in general and in particular were not at all afraid to share their difficulties. I encouraged study partners and allowed for time in class for them to team up to work things out with one another. I would not formally set up research buddies until the following semester, but the work that they did collaboratively, I believe, was invaluable to their process and confidence.

The final weeks of the semester were stressful for all of us. Some students had hit more than a few hitches and the usual meltdowns occurred, sometimes simultaneously with the snow and ice we were experiencing, along with colds and flu and general mental and physical fatigue. More than once the professor and I were reminded by the students that they had other classes they had to focus on, too. Students are not widgets; they cannot, nor should they be, manipulated or intimidated. My one requirement for working with them was "do your work and do it well." The unique position of the librarian in the classroom is that while I am also responsible for student learning in the class, I am also able to be a fuller support system for them as well. I did not grade their final projects, though I would provide feedback to the professor. I was committed to seeing them through the process, right to the end, which continued into the spring semester, after the formal class had ended.

When the class presented their theses in the spring, that year, I remember feeling not only a sense of pride in their achievements, but also a sense of accomplishment at the successful collaboration that had unfolded throughout that semester. Some of that success was hard won: as the semester wore on, it was difficult to gauge what we might term as "success" because the class was not, as no class ever is, monolithic in any way. Yes, they were all senior English majors, but how they all got to be there was a circuitous route for some, and for others, more straightforward. The embedded librarian plans, but strict mandates only straitjacket a process that must be organic and tailored to the class you are with at the moment. Zoe, one of my hardest working though struggling students, thanked me publicly after presenting her thesis: "I want to thank our librarian, Michelle, for her help through the process. She was like my best friend for four months!" Less enthusiastic though no less sincere, other students expressed the same sentiments that day and it brought home the value of what I had attempted to do with a startling clarity. It was a day when more than just a few faculty became both intrigued and surprised that we, as librarians, were capable, and more importantly, it was through student testimonials that they realized this. A long road, an odyssey, but well worth it, and of course, always growing and evolving.

FINAL THOUGHTS

As clichéd as it sounds (and it does), the road to embedded librarianship is a marathon, not a sprint. A librarian's success in the embedded classroom will depend on any number of variables, and so it is good to define what your idea of "success" will be. I was thrilled just to be in the classroom after so many fits and starts. Once there, I could unfold my plan of (collaborative) learning. *Not* being in the classroom left me with the frustrating one-shot instructions that were barely scratching the surface of what good instruction could be. The term *odyssey* is not one that I chose lightly. It accurately describes the process of becoming more of the librarian that I was meant to be.

NOTE

1. Robert Kegan, *In Over Our Heads: The Metal Demands of Modern Life* (Cambridge, MA: Harvard University Press, 1994), 42.

RESOURCES

Boyd, Melaine. "Library-Faculty Relations—Gaps and Bridges: Connecting within Our Communities." ACRL WNY/O Chapter Spring Conference Friday, May 4, 2007.

Brown, Jennifer Diane, and Thomas Scott Duke. "Librarian and Faculty Collaborative Instruction: A Phenomenological Self-Study." *Research Strategies* 20, no. 3 (2005): 171–90.

Cook, Douglas, and Ryan Sittler, eds. *Practical Pedagogy for Library Instructors: 17 Innovative Strategies to Improve Student Learning.* Association of College and Research Libraries, 2008.

Kegan, Robert. *In Over Our Heads: The Mental Demands of Modern Life.* Cambridge, MA: Harvard University Press, 1994.

Knapp, Jeffrey A., Nicholas J. Rowland, and Eric P. Charles. "Retaining Students by Embedding Librarians into Undergraduate Research Experiences." *Reference Services Review* 42, no. 1 (2014): 129–47.

Kolb, Alice Y., and David A. Kolb. "Learning Styles and Learning Spaces: Enhancing Experiential Learning in Higher Education." *Academy of Management Learning & Education* 4, no. 2 (2005): 193–212.

Kotter, Wade R. "Bridging the Great Divide: Improving Relations between Librarians and Classroom Faculty." *The Journal of Academic Librarianship* 25, no. 4 (1999): 294–303.

Murray, Tara E. "Applying Traditional Librarianship to New Roles for Special Librarians." *Journal of Library Administration* 54, no. 4 (2014): 327–36.

Peacock, Judith A. "Teaching Skills for Teaching Librarians: Postcards from the Edge of the Educational Paradigm." *Australian Academic & Research Libraries* 32, no. 1 (2001): 26–42.

Rader, Hannelore B. "Building Faculty-Librarian Partnerships to Prepare Students for Information Fluency." *College & Research Libraries News* 65, no. 2 (2004): 74–77.

Winner, Marian C. "Librarians as Partners in the Classroom: An Increasing Imperative." *Reference Services Review* 26, no. 1 (1998): 25–29.

12
In Retrospect

For last year's words belong to last year's language
and next year's words await another voice.
And to make an end is to make a new beginning.

—T. S. Eliot

WHEN I ENTERED THE HUGE, HEAVY DOORS OF THE CASTLE, the crowning glory, with reason, of our small, suburban campus, I felt the excitement—it was palpable. It was "Thesis Week" at our university, a weeklong celebration and culmination of final senior projects proudly, and sometimes anxiously and worriedly, presented to the campus community, family, and friends. It is what we all wait for and what graduating seniors look forward to as it signals both an end and a beginning for all of us.

Through the doors I could hear happily raised voices, the persistent "thrum" of the excitement that everyone felt before the start of the Senior Thesis presentations. I had arrived just a tad early, though most of the seats were taken. I sat in the back, near a table full of fancy snacks and cold beverages for the audience. The English department faculty, all in attendance, sat together, waved, and alternately mouthed "good luck" to students, who were dressed in the clothes of the professionals they were on the verge of becoming. I have been on this campus for quite some time now, and yet I have never tired of this tradition, this showcasing of such hard work and the culmination of knowledge and the feeling of esprit de corps that we very clearly all felt.

But as I looked back to January, after the welcome and needed holiday stretch, it all looked and felt so different. Students came back to campus, glad to have the fall semester behind them, but anxious, to say the least, of the fact that their final drafts for the thesis were due the second week in March. Class was finished, and we would no longer be meeting as a group, and in so many ways, this was when the hard work, for me, and the students really began. With drafts in hand, copiously marked up by their professors, much to their dismay, they began, one by one, making appointments with me. There were some days when it was difficult to get through to students who clung to inappropriate sources or not fully realized assertions, because they were mentally fatigued at even the thought of any changes, let alone major ones in a paper that they thought they had already worked far too long on. They had head colds, then I had chest colds, they cried, had mini-meltdowns, crises of confidence; they simply just wanted to be done already and were sick and tired of the subject matter. There were a few, but just a few, who did not have to make many changes. I assured them that this was all part of the process, knowing all the while that they just would not understand until it was over; then they really would not even be able to remember what they'd just gone through!

Finally, the appointments slowed down as students began to find a rhythm in the revision process—a crucial element in the writing of a final project and the opportunity, as I continuously told them, to literally "revision" the paper—to look at it with fresh eyes. For the most part, I realized that much of the major information searching was done. The few who were given feedback on a new direction for their papers needed to start the search over for appropriate research, and others needed a variety of different things, but I think, no, *I know* that the majority of them needed emotional support through the process. Without class as the glue that held us together, many students expressed a feeling akin to "free fall" —the feeling that they were well and truly on their own and alone in the process of finalizing their paper. And it occurred to me, not for the first time, that the reason I find embedded librarianship so valuable is because I can fully support students both in and out of the classroom with a continuity that is seamless: that I can faithfully see them through the very beginning of the process right to the very end. It is, in my opinion, a privileged and unique position from which to work.

Instinctively, I had never been a proponent of the one-shot instruction class, and as an academic librarian had struggled consistently with a practice that seemed to fit many faculty members' ideas of what was "enough" instruction for a class. That left me with the feeling that I never was in the position to see the educational life cycle; that I was almost always meeting students at the same developmental stage and could not see what happened before or after that stage.

As I sat in the ornate room with the bright lights, among all of the people who had invested in my students' success—parents, friends, and family—I thought how multilayered the process really is. That these students had lives beyond the one that I saw on campus and in the classroom; they had people who loved them and were cheering them on. The benefit of being close, being *there* during the struggle and during the celebration is that we can see the student as a whole person, holistically, which renews and reaffirms our place in the educational ecosystem.

One by one the students took the podium, looked out upon a sea of friendly faces, and began to hold forth on the topics they'd been working on assiduously for months on end. Some took deep breaths. Some faltered, at the beginning, but then gained equilibrium and flow. The one student who said, in near tears, "I can't do this," did just that.

The president of the university, a tall and regal woman, sat beside me, her chin tilted upward over the many heads in front of us. She was smiling broadly, especially when one of the students presented her thesis on the *Wizard of Oz*. Later, it was said, she mentioned to someone that it was one of her favorite presentations that week and I remembered how she adjusted her skirt and leaned in to hear better. I passed that on to Megan, the student who presented, and she beamed.

The celebratory bottles of champagne for the students were opened at the end, to great applause. This is a tradition that marks the formal end of all thesis requirements. One student who struggled desperately during the year, with her two sons beside her, had tears in her eyes as she embraced me. "I really did it," she said, almost unbelievably, then: "Thank you for believing in me!"

I slipped away with the celebration in full swing. My job with these students was complete and I was already looking to the next group. As I summed up my own experiences I asked myself a question:

Can students live without us?

My answer was: Probably.

Emboldened by my own honesty, I asked another:

Are they, their work, and their experience better for our involvement in the life cycle of the educational process?

That answer was easy and came readily to mind: Most definitely, *yes*.

Index